# ROUTLEDGE LIBRARY EDITIONS: LIBRARY AND INFORMATION SCIENCE

Volume 69

# THE PUBLIC LIBRARY IN THE BIBLIOGRAPHIC NETWORK

# THE PUBLIC LIBRARY IN THE BIBLIOGRAPHIC NETWORK

Edited by
BETTY J. TUROCK

LONDON AND NEW YORK

First published in 1986 by The Haworth Press, Inc.

This edition first published in 2020
by Routledge
2 Park Square, Milton Park, Abingdon, Oxon OX14 4RN

and by Routledge
52 Vanderbilt Avenue, New York, NY 10017

*Routledge is an imprint of the Taylor & Francis Group, an informa business*

© 1986 The Haworth Press, Inc.

All rights reserved. No part of this book may be reprinted or reproduced or utilised in any form or by any electronic, mechanical, or other means, now known or hereafter invented, including photocopying and recording, or in any information storage or retrieval system, without permission in writing from the publishers.

*Trademark notice*: Product or corporate names may be trademarks or registered trademarks, and are used only for identification and explanation without intent to infringe.

*British Library Cataloguing in Publication Data*
A catalogue record for this book is available from the British Library

ISBN: 978-0-367-34616-4 (Set)
ISBN: 978-0-429-34352-0 (Set) (ebk)
ISBN: 978-0-367-42106-9 (Volume 69) (hbk)
ISBN: 978-0-367-42115-1 (Volume 69) (pbk)
ISBN: 978-0-367-82187-6 (Volume 69) (ebk)

**Publisher's Note**
The publisher has gone to great lengths to ensure the quality of this reprint but points out that some imperfections in the original copies may be apparent.

**Disclaimer**
The publisher has made every effort to trace copyright holders and would welcome correspondence from those they have been unable to trace.

# The Public Library in the Bibliographic Network

Betty J. Turock
Editor

The Haworth Press
New York • London

*The Public Library in the Bibliographic Network* has also been published as *Resource Sharing and Information Networks*, Volume 3, Number 2, Spring/Summer 1986.

© 1986 by The Haworth Press, Inc. All rights reserved. No part of this book may be reproduced or utilized in any form or by any means, electronic or mechanical, including photocopying, microfilm and recording, or by any information storage and retrieval system, without permission in writing from the publisher. Printed in the United States of America.

The Haworth Press, Inc., 12 West 32 Street, New York, NY 10001
EUROSPAN/Haworth, 3 Henrietta Street, London WC2E 8LU England

**Library of Congress Cataloging-in-Publication Data**

The Public library in the bibliographic network.

   Includes bibliographies.
   1. Library information networks—United States. 2. Public libraries—United States—Automation. 3. Bibliographical services—United States. I. Turock, Betty J.
Z674.8.P83      1986      027.473      86-14915
ISBN 0-86656-595-7

# The Public Library in the Bibliographic Network

Resource Sharing and Information Networks
Volume 3, Number 2

## CONTENTS

| | |
|---|---|
| **Editor's Note** | 1 |
| **Foreword** | 3 |
|     *Donald J. Sager* | |
| Cost and Benefits of OCLC Use in Small and Medium Size Public Libraries | 9 |
|     *Linda G. Bills* | |
|   The System and the Libraries | 9 |
|   The OCLC Experimental Project | 10 |
|   Project Strategies | 10 |
|   Library Clusters | 16 |
|   Public Access Terminals | 19 |
|   Cataloging | 19 |
|   Interlibrary Loan | 24 |
|   Cost of OCLC | 31 |
|   The Decision | 31 |
|   Conclusions | 33 |
| **The Kewanee Public Library Votes Yes on OCLC** | 35 |
|     *Harriet Conklin* | |
|   Joining the Experiment | 35 |
|   RECON and ILL | 36 |
|   OCLC Stays in Kewanee | 37 |
|   Cluster Fails | 37 |
|   The Negative Side of Membership | 38 |

## We'll Wait and See — 41
### *Thomas H. Ballard*

| | |
|---|---|
| The Plainfield Public Library | 41 |
| The Union County and New Jersey Situation | 42 |
| Plainfield's Position | 44 |
| Circulation and Interlibrary Loan | 44 |
| OCLC and Plainfield | 47 |
| Present and Future Cost Comparisons | 50 |
| Other More Speculative Considerations | 51 |
| Is Plainfield a Good Neighbor? | 53 |
| Resource Sharing | 53 |
| Conclusion | 55 |

## A WLN Dilemma — 57
### *Mark A. Nesse*

| | |
|---|---|
| Initiating a Bibliographic Network in Washington | 57 |
| Adding Services | 58 |
| RECON, Cataloging and the Network | 59 |
| The COM Catalog | 61 |
| Online Circulation and Integrated Systems | 62 |
| The RFP | 63 |
| Dilemma Resolved | 66 |
| Decision Reviewed | 68 |

## Linking CLSI and UTLAS to Meet Local Needs — 71
### *Polly Coe*

| | |
|---|---|
| Deciding the Priorities | 72 |
| Costing the Project | 73 |
| Going Out for Bids | 73 |
| Shared Cataloging Via a Network | 75 |

## Present and Future Network Base for New Mexico's Public Libraries — 77
### *Ed Sayre*

| | |
|---|---|
| Resource Sharing in New Mexico | 78 |
| The Los Alamos Connection | 79 |
| OCLC and RECON | 81 |
| Effectiveness and Efficiency | 82 |
| Contributions and the Future | 83 |

**Networking at the Principal Public Library in Rhode Island: A Decade of Change**     85
    *Annalee M. Bundy*

Online Circulation, Acquisitions and Public Access Catalog     85
MINI-MARC for Cataloging and Card Production     87
RECON for Greater Public Access     88
OCLC Re-Enters     89

# EDITOR'S NOTE

The Public Library Association's Task Force on Network Relations, one of several established in 1982-1983 by President Donald J. Sager "to open some new doors on tangible problems" was charged with reviewing the current status of public library participation in online bibliographic networks and developing recommendations to stimulate greater utilization and participation in the design of services beneficial to their operations. During the first two years of Task Force work, I served as Chair. Hildred Shelton, Director of the Pittsylvania County (VA) Library, followed me in 1984.

At its organizational meeting the Task Force established a three pronged investigatory process to meet the charge. It included holding an open hearing, commissioning a series of case studies, and conducting a survey of network participants and nonparticipants. The goal was to bring the products of these processes to the attention of the profession through a series of publications.

The first phase, the Open Hearing, was held June 23, 1983 at the American Library Association's Annual Conference. An analysis and synthesis of the presentations, testimonies and written statements was published previously in the Winter, 1984 issue of *Public Library Quarterly*. Following the session, the Task Force identified

---

The Editor of this special issue, Betty J. Turock, is a member of the faculty at Rutgers University's School of Communication, Information and Library Studies, where she coordinates the management concentration. The public library is the primary focus of her research. Until 1980, Dr. Turock served as Assistant Director of the Rochester and Monroe (NY) Public Library System. Formerly she was Assistant Director, then Director of the Montclair (NJ) Public Library.

© 1986 by The Haworth Press, Inc. All rights reserved.

libraries and authors for the second phase of activity, i.e., preparation of the case studies depicting decisions about membership in bibliographic networks.

The final report on the third phase of Task Force work, "A National Investigation of The Public Library in the Bibliographic Network", is scheduled for presentation at the Public Library Association's national conference in St. Louis on April 3, 1986. At that time findings from all three phases will be brought together in commentary and recommendations.

It is hoped that the case studies presented in this issue of *RSIN* will help to answer questions surrounding decisions about joining bibliographic networks and move public librarians toward guidelines for that determination.

The libraries described by the authors are of varying sizes and located in different geographic regions. Reasons for joining or not joining bibliographic networks are outlined as well as the process of decision-making. Uses of the networks, their costs, including initial and ongoing expenses, and staffing needs are detailed. Expected and unexpected, desirable and undesirable results are highlighted.

In the Foreword Don Sager summarizes the current status of participation in bibliographic networks and draws some conclusions about its import for public libraries. It is fitting that the word foreword has as one of its meanings advocating policy in the direction of progress. Since Sager began the Task force and its activity, it is also fitting that he set the scene for one of its major reports to the profession.

*Betty J. Turock*
*Rutgers University*

# Foreword

I have come to the belief that despite all the lip service given to interlibrary cooperation, resource sharing and commonly accepted standards, public librarians remain rugged individualists bound together by a mutual dislike of uniformity. Nothing is more revealing of this attitude than the public library's role in bibliographic networks, and this issue contains a good cross section of opinion on that subject.

Each of the articles approaches the issue of participation in networks from a different perspective. Linda Bills underlines the value of participation by even the smallest library, but acknowledges the relatively high cost. Harriet Conklin's experience supports those conclusions. Tom Ballard expresses a willingness to share his library's bibliographic records and resources, but believes the cost is too great compared with other alternatives, and of limited value to his institution and community. Mark Nesse, on the other side of the nation, arrived at a similar conclusion based on somewhat different experience and grounds. Ed Sayre feels that despite the high costs of network participation, there are a variety of benefits which offset, at least in part, some of these costs. Nonetheless, he does have some doubts about the state library agency's justification for subsidizing these costs for small libraries. Polly Coe also finds some value in network participation, but only as long as that value exceeds actual cost for her library. Finally, Annalee Bundy casts a skeptical eye on network participation, only using it because of state subsidy for interlibrary loan purposes.

Of course, each of these individuals has made the right decision for his/her own library and community, carefully reached after analyzing the costs and needs. I am confident that each of these administrators can thoroughly defend that decision in whatever forum they may enter. The question I raise is who speaks for the national interest in this matter? Is it in the national interest that a public library can elect not to share information on its holdings, and avoid responsibility for financially contributing to the national networks. Interestingly, several of the authors who do not belong or fully participate in the bibliographic networks state they have value for certain types of libraries, usually citing the larger library as the probable beneficiary, and as an institution that can best afford participation. Yet, the past three national surveys of public libraries undertaken by the National Center for Educational Statistics (NCES) clearly reveal these institutions are experiencing the most serious declines in revenue, when their income is adjusted to reflect inflation, and they are among the least likely to use interlibrary loan. Those same surveys reveal that it is the smaller and medium sized library that is more likely to use interlibrary loan, and has experienced the most real growth in income.

I can agree that it may seem unreasonable for the citizens of Plainfield or Everett to pay additional taxes so that the citizens of Peoria can have the benefit of the holdings of the other libraries. I can even accept the fact that the citizens of Peoria are unlikely to even know this is possible, much less want to make use of this opportunity. But as a member of a profession which presumably is committed to freedom of access and the preservation and advancement of knowledge, I feel an obligation to ensure the *opportunity* to share bibliographic information is preserved for all libraries and communities. That is a cost which may have to be shared, even though all do not equally benefit. I further feel that responsible professionals would do their best to promote public awareness of this opportunity.

As a library administrator, I can understand the reluctance of any responsible manager to spend hard won tax funds to catalog resources on a bibliographic network when there are more economical alternatives. However, by failing to participate in that network and sharing holdings information, the residents of that community lose the opportunity for broader access to resources, and that is something on which no dollar value can be placed. It is similar to weighing the difference between an adequate education, compared to excellence. It becomes much more difficult when your own child is affected.

Participation in a network has a cost; no question about it. It can be argued that until pricing is adjusted to permit small and medium public libraries (or large libraries for that matter) to afford participation on an equitable basis, it would be best to remain outside the membership. However, it can also be argued that until public libraries take a greater role in bibliographic networks, the pricing and other philosophies of those networks are not likely to change.

Several years ago, when I proposed the creation of a task force on bibliographic networks in the Public Library Association, I was motivated by the knowledge that public libraries constituted only a very small percentage of network membership. In 1982, only 434 public libraries were members of the three major networks. I'm pleased there has been some progress. The most recent annual report issued by the Online Computer Library Center (OCLC), for example, noted there were 718 public libraries who were voting members. I'm also aware that many public libraries participate in processing centers or share their holdings through various state and regional networks, and these find their way into national networks. Nonetheless, the percentage is still woefully low, compared to the potential. The latest NCES national survey, undertaken in 1982, and just released this year, reports 8,597 public libraries, with 70,573 outlets.

That same survey also includes, for the first time, information regarding public library use of automation. I had the opportunity to serve as an advisor to the NCES when they developed that portion of the survey form, and I was particularly interested in determining the use public libraries made of computers for cataloging and interlibrary loan. Sadly, the survey revealed that only a relatively small percentage of public libraries used computers at all. Eight percent used computers for interlibrary loan, and it was the most frequently cited computer application. All the other functions were considerably below this.

Judging by exhibits and programs at state and national conferences, that situation is rapidly changing, and more recent surveys give evidence that microcomputers are increasing in all sizes of libraries as cost decreases, library applications proliferate, and the profession becomes better trained. That trend has potential to improve public library participation in networks. Whether it helps, or leads more libraries to abandon network participation remains to be seen.

With a microcomputer the local library can perform simple cataloging, administer circulation, access online reference databases, and handle a host of other administrative functions. The potential also exists for the local library to upload its bibliographic records and other databases into regional, state, and national networks to further improve resource sharing. Several of the articles in this issue give evidence that this is not taking place. Instead, local libraries are retaining their own holdings and other databases, either because there is no vehicle or standard protocol for transfer, or for lack of any motivation, or perhaps both.

It is my belief that public libraries will certainly increase their use of computers, primarily microcomputers, and while there will be some cooperative applications through local area networking, there will not be a dramatic increase in public library participation in bibliographic networks unless the state library agencies and/or the networks take some greater initiative. This might involve further state subsidy or network pricing changes. Many states are developing statewide union catalogs, and the networks are frequently used as a mechanism for retrospective conversion. Unfortunately, the networks are not always used for ongoing maintenance of local library holdings.

At least one of the networks has taken some actions which hold potential for improving the public library's role. OCLC has established an advisory panel on public libraries, and it has increased the number of microcomputer applications which are available through state and regional networks. The hardware and software is economical enough for even smaller public libraries, and they have the option of accessing the online union catalog through dial up. OCLC has also promoted low cost union catalog services which allow local public libraries to participate without formally joining OCLC or their state or regional network. Recent controversy regarding the copyright of the OCLC database has muddied the water, and caused some regional networks and states to delay in fully utilizing OCLC while they explored other options. Nonetheless, progress has occurred in the matter of third party use of OCLC records, and that should lead to restoration of contractual negotiations. The other major bibliographic networks have also continued to evolve, and are more actively marketing their services.

While this journal provides an excellent range of opinion on public library participation in bibliographic networks, it does not answer the question of how these institutions can ever effectively share their resources if they do not participate. Some of the authors question whether this is important, or worth the high cost. As evident in this foreword, I believe it is important, and that we cannot afford to deny access on a national basis to local holdings. While there may be other technological means of achieving this access in the future, the national bibliographic networks provide the only means of achieving this at the present and the near future.

Earlier, I asked who represents the national interest in this matter. Of course, it is the profession. Ultimately, we must examine whether public libraries have the responsibility to share resources on a national basis, and should contribute to the support of some efficient means to facilitate access. The editor has performed an excellent service in selecting authors who represent a diversity of opinion on this subject. When we reach a consensus in the profession, then some progress will occur.

*Donald J. Sager, Director*
*Milwaukee Public Library*
*Milwaukee, Wisconsin*

# Cost and Benefits of OCLC Use in Small and Medium Size Public Libraries

Linda G. Bills

From January of 1980 to December of 1982, the Illinois Valley Library System (IVLS) and its participating libraries conducted an LSCA funded experimental project in OCLC use. Although the purpose of the project was to examine the costs and benefits of OCLC in small and medium size libraries of all types, 20 of the 33 participants were public libraries. During the project both subjective and objective studies were conducted to measure OCLC use and its effects on the libraries and the System. This article summarizes those studies. Complete documentation is available in a series of reports from the Illinois State Library (Bills, 1982-1984).

## *THE SYSTEM AND THE LIBRARIES*

The Illinois Valley Library System is one of eighteen state funded agencies in Illinois whose purpose is to provide services to their participating libraries and to promote cooperation among them. IVLS is a multitype which currently has 73 participating libraries, 35 of which are public. It includes a large urban center (Peoria), suburban areas, and rural farming/industrial communities.

The System's relationship with its participating libraries can best be explained by it role statement:

> The role of the Illinois Valley Library System shall be to help existing libraries reach their full potential by facilitating cooperative activities between libraries and by providing services that cannot be provided through maximum local effort.

---

Linda G. Bills, OCLC Project Director, Illinois Valley Library System, Pekin, IL 61554.
The project described was funded by an LSCA grant under the auspices of the Illinois State Library. The article is based on a series of reports published by the Illinois State Library.

© 1986 by The Haworth Press, Inc. All rights reserved.

The System supplies delivery among libraries, interlibrary loan, back-up reference, films and talking books, among other services. A staff of professional librarians, employed by the System, serve as consultants. Participant libraries agree to share resources according to the Illinois Interlibrary Loan Code, to meet the primary needs of their own clientele and to maintain the level of library support that existed at the time they joined the System. In addition, all public libraries are required to participate in reciprocal borrowing.

## *THE OCLC EXPERIMENTAL PROJECT*

In 1977, a special Task Force at IVLS searched the literature to determine the costs and benefits of various alternative proposals for automated resource sharing. This search revealed a dearth of information. What was available dealt almost exclusively with larger units of service, especially research libraries and large academic institutions.

The Task Force recommended, therefore, that a project be undertaken as an experiment to use OCLC for local resource sharing among small units of service. An LSCA grant designed to do this was funded by the Illinois State Library. The focus of the project was to provide increased access to resources by building a data base of local holdings that could be shared among area libraries as well as with libraries throughout Illinois and the nation. The use of OCLC as a cataloging tool was a complementary process whose costs and benefits were also examined.

## *PROJECT STRATEGIES*

During the project, staff of small and medium size libraries used OCLC terminals located either in their own library or in a neighboring library. Host libraries were those which had terminals and printers throughout the project. Guest libraries had no permanent terminal or printer, but used one in a host library. Together a host and its guests formed a cluster. Each library had its own profile and OCLC symbol. The staff were trained in the use of both the cataloging and the interlibrary loan subsystems of OCLC. Other subsystems, such as acquisitions and serials control, were not introduced as part of the project.

The grant reduced the financial burden to the libraries participating in this experiment. All OCLC equipment and use charges were subsidized for two years. The only payment most libraries made was a per title refund to the project of the amount it cost to catalog before OCLC was in place. Interlibrary loan charges, retrospective conversion, profiling, terminal maintenance, service fees and installation were paid for by the project.

In order to build an online database of local holding symbols in OCLC, every participating library was required to update records to reflect all the books they owned which were published in 1975 or later. Staff time and travel required to do this work were not reimbursed to the library; it constituted part of their local effort. Some of the libraries, in addition to what was required, converted earlier titles or included audiovisual materials and sound recordings. Work in retrospective conversion began in December of 1980. Most of it was completed by December of the next year. During the project, in addition to the fixed terminals, six were shifted among most of the project libraries so each could have a terminal available for patron use for six months. These public access arrangements were intended to increase patron awareness of OCLC and library networks.

*OCLC Costs*. The prices charged for OCLC services vary from network to network. The ILLINET network office is totally supported by the Illinois State Library, so none of the costs for its staff, equipment or other expenses fall on the membership. There are no network, entrance fees or membership fees. As a result, through ILLINET members paid the OCLC charges plus a share of the telecommunications costs for the Illinois OCLC network. Table I summarizes the cost of OCLC use on a dedicated line during the project.

The acronym FTU means first time use, the basic cataloging fee charged by OCLC the first time a library uses a record; there is no charge for later uses. ILLINET did not begin charging a modem fee until March, 1982. It was pro-rated for previous months from July, 1981 to cover existing telecommunications' bills. Until July, 1984 ILLINET distributed telecommunications costs based on OCLC use.

In addition, each library had certain start up expenses which included, at the time of the project:

| | |
|---|---|
| Terminal purchase | $3,700 |
| Modem installation | 148 |
| Installation of electrical outlets | Varied |
| Profile costs | Varied |

TABLE I

COSTS OF OCLC USE IN ILLINET
Dedicated Terminal

| OCLC Charges | 1980/81 | 1981/82 | 1982/83 |
|---|---|---|---|
| Use Charges | | | |
| Cataloging FTU | $1.36 | $1.40 | $1.46 |
| Cards (per card) | .042 | .042 | .0455 |
| Retrospective Conversion | | | |
| Prime time | .80 | .80 | .85–.91 |
| Non-Prime time | .05 | .10–.15 | .18–.22 |
| ILL request initiation | .95 | 1.20 | 1.28 |
| Annual Fees | | | |
| Terminal maintenance | 396.00 | 432.00 | 486.00 |
| Terminal service fee | | 300.00 | 318.00 |
| Modem fee | | 336.00 | 600.00 |
| Telecommunications Charges | | | |
| Per cataloging FTU | .45 | .60 | .75 |
| Per ILL request | — | — | — |

The strategy was to relieve libraries of nearly all these expenses and let them experience OCLC use without having to commit funds. At the end of the project, when they were asked whether they would keep or drop OCLC, it was hoped that their decisions would be based on their experiences in the previous two years rather than on any large, past financial investment.

*Project Libraries.* When financial support ended in June of 1982, each participant had to decide whether to maintain the OCLC connection at its own expense. Twelve of the 20 decided to do so. The public libraries in the project ranged considerably in size and circumstances. The largest, the Peoria Public Library, serves a population of 126,000 and has four branches besides its large downtown facility. The smallest, Mason Memorial Library in Buda, serves a rural town of 700. Table II gives a few statistics for these libraries.

Staff size is given in full time equivalents (FTEs), with the number of staff members having MLS degrees shown in parentheses. Annual acquisitions are based on 1982 figures. Annual ILL is for 1980, before extensive use of the OCLC subsystem.

The experience of the libraries' staffs varied greatly. In one case the librarian had worked in a pre-professional capacity as an OCLC copy cataloger. In a few others the director and/or some staff members had recently taken courses that included an introduction to

OCLC and MARC. One of the participating libraries had used OCLC for interlibrary loan as part of the nationwide test of that subsystem, but had never used it for cataloging. In the larger libraries, several directors had investigated OCLC as a potential tool from the administrative point of view. Overall, however, the level of hands-on experience by directors and staff was low; most had never been exposed to OCLC or automated systems of any kind. Their understanding of the way OCLC functioned, what it would do for their libraries, and how it might affect their operations was based on information received from the ILVS. In many cases, their agreement to participate was an act of faith in response to the System's recommendation.

In the majority of the project public libraries, staff were not only unfamiliar with automation, they also were not aware of many facets of cataloging that are central to understanding MARC tagging and using OCLC records. Cards for their catalogs were obtained from vendors or typed in-house. If CIP was available, it was used with very little alteration. The most frequent changes were in class numbers or subject heading to conform with the existing catalog.

*Expectations*. During interviews in May of 1981, librarians were asked to describe what their expectations for the project were. Their

TABLE II

Public Library Full Participants in the OCLC Project

| Library | Population | Income | Staff (MLS) | Volumes | Annual Acq | Annual ILL |
|---|---|---|---|---|---|---|
| Alpha Park | 21,800 | 297,557 | 11.9 [4] | 34,900 | 5,000 | 1,200 |
| Ayer | 2,400 | 28,000 | 1.2 [-] | 12,100 | 380 | 150 |
| Bradford | 924 | 6,000 | .4 [-] | 5,000 | 171 | 139 |
| Dunlap | 4,700 | 72,600 | 2.5 [1] | 14,800 | 2,600 | 1,000 |
| Elmwood | 2,700 | 60,000 | 1.2 [-] | 9,500 | 500 | 280 |
| Fondulac | 13,500 | 254,600 | 9.5 [3] | 34,019 | 4,000 | 750 |
| Galva | 3,700 | 53,343 | 3.4 [-] | 17,700 | 1,500 | 780 |
| Henry | 2,700 | 30,600 | 1.2 [-] | 16,700 | 800 | 610 |
| Illinois Prairie | 18,000 | 181,800 | 4.7 [1] | 70,000 | 3,600 | 1,000 |
| Kewanee | 16,400 | 148,200 | 8.9 [3] | 58,000 | 3,400 | 750 |
| Lillie M. Evans | 1,700 | 33,600 | 2.1 [-] | 16,200 | 800 | 290 |
| Mackinaw | 2,800 | 36,800 | 2.1 [1] | 12,500 | 900 | 520 |
| Mason Memorial | 700 | 250,000 | .4 [-] | 7,000 | 800 | 60 |
| Morton | 14,200 | 218,500 | 6.1 [1] | 30,000 | 2,000 | 1,500 |
| Neponset | 1,000 | 15,900 | 1.4 [-] | 13,900 | 600 | 50 |
| Pekin | 34,000 | 383,000 | 16.0 [5] | 73,000 | 5,200 | 1,200 |
| Peoria | 124,160 | 1,400,000 | 112.0 [6] | 451,000 | 19,000 | 1,700 |
| Toulon | 1,400 | 9,700 | .5 [-] | 7,000 | 40 | 124 |
| Washington | 20,000 | 184,000 | 8.7 [3] | 33,500 | 1,700 | 1,100 |
| Wyoming | 1,600 | 6,000 | .4 [-] | 5,100 | 140 | 300 |

responses generally fell into two groups—professional and personal. The major professional, or library-oriented, expectations were the anticipation of new/enhanced user services and concern for how OCLC could be supported after the project. The more personal anticipations highlighted some of the problems on introducing OCLC to librarians with no previous experience. They included:

> Anxiety about whether they could handle the technology and learn the necessary skills.
>
> Concern about staff resistance to the changes and how the staff would adapt.
>
> Concern for the management, safety and housing of the equipment.

The anxiety over handling new technology focused on the anticipation of personal inadequacy because of inexperience rather than fear of dehumanizing influences. Only five directors said that they knew what to expect because of previous experience.

*Profiling.* New OCLC members must create a profile which describes the format and print characteristics of their catalog cards. In some networks this is mediated by network staff who help the library fill out the necessary technical forms. In the project, it was mediated by system staff who, in turn, were helped by ILLINET. Each library had its own profile so that each library would have its own OCLC library symbol. Public library profiles were particularly complex when compared to academic libraries, for example, because holdings were broken into collections and subcollections such as juvenile, easy, picture books, young adult, mystery, large print, etc.

The chief difficulty with the original profiling was the lack of familiarity in libraries with the terms needed for an exact description of catalog practices. Also because of lack of experience with OCLC, many librarians had difficulty in understanding the options available. As a result, profiling generally had two stages—the first developed a profile that reproduced the library's existing practices. About a year later, having developed a hands-on understanding of OCLC options, profiles were rewritten to take advantage of those options.

*Training.* The project director and her assistant, both of whom had MLS degrees and technical service backgrounds, had responsibility for training for OCLC use. Throughout the project, training was provided on three levels. Workshops were designed to cover the basics of each OCLC operation in small group sessions of six to eight people. After the workshop, project staff were available, if desired by the library, to work with trainees one-to-one at terminals for about half a day. Finally, all library staff members were encouraged to call the project office as problems arose, or to check records they wished to put in their save files, or if unclear information appeared on the screen.

The general philosophy in all the training sessions was to teach participants what they must know to handle 90 percent of their materials. Most staff members learned basic OCLC editing quickly, without further training because most libraries made very few changes to cataloging records. The changes made fell into two areas, call numbers or subject headings. The staff members who required the most reinforcement after the initial training sessions were those with the fewest books to catalog.

Because the hit rate on OCLC was very high for the libraries—even in audiovisual materials—very little original cataloging was needed during the project. Over the total two years of the project, 930 items in the 29 new OCLC libraries of all types needed original input. This was .32 percent of all cataloging, retrospective conversion and reclassification.

One negative influence at this time was the documentation received from OCLC and the network. Before library staff had any substantial introduction to what operations with OCLC would be like, they received many boxes of manuals, bulletins and other documents. These gave the impression that automation was far too complex and time-consuming for libraries with few staff members. Simply organizing all the paper they received initially and continued to receive in batches was daunting to many project participants. In some cases, it was merely piled in a corner unopened. Even after they had learned to use OCLC and understood the role of the various manuals and communications, 59.3 percent of the directors reported in interviews that this documentation was burdensome and overwhelming.

By the 1981 interviews with all library directors, the original anxiety about handling the technology had proved completely unfounded. When librarians were asked to relate the disadvantages of OCLC use, none of them responded that the technology was too complex to learn or too difficult to handle. Two librarians said that the need to learn new skills and train new staff was a disadvantage. On the other hand, increased job satisfaction on the part of staff was volunteered as a benefit by 40 percent of the directors.

Our experience and the reports from library directors led us to a number of conclusions about the implementation of OCLC in small and medium size public libraries where staff has little or no previous experience with OCLC. They include that:

1. Training can be brief, i.e., conducted in as little as two days if it is focused on what is most essential, if it can be backed up by brief, relevant written summaries or memory aids, and if telephone consultation is easily available. It is not profitable to attempt comprehensive training.
2. The OCLC display format and terminal design presented barriers to easy learning, but soon became accepted.
3. It is invaluable to have trainers/teachers with a strong local affiliation. We were associated with the Illinois Valley Library System, a known and trusted source of advice. The group of libraries being trained was small enough that personal contacts could be sustained. This sense of availability encouraged participants to contact the project office with minor problems which often prevented major ones from developing. This strong local support became less important later as libraries became self-reliant OCLC users, but it was essential in the initial stages.

## *LIBRARY CLUSTERS*

One of the major objectives of the project was to determine whether sharing an OCLC terminal among several libraries could significantly cut costs and yet provide acceptable service. The clusters were arranged so that two to five libraries in close geographic proximity shared a terminal.

There are several general environmental factors that made clustering attractive in IVLS. First, the system maintains a regular delivery service to all area libraries. These deliveries provided an easy means for transferring OCLC information, such as printouts. Second, library staff in the system were accustomed to working together on local and system-wide projects. Finally, the participants knew from the start that their use of OCLC in the project would involve sharing a terminal. Although the structure of their cluster was not clearly defined in the beginning, any library that joined accepted clustering as a part of their commitment.

There were some conditions in project libraries which made clustering difficult. One major problem was the time spent by the guest library staff members away from their own libraries. In most clusters, the largest library was the host. The guest libraries, in many cases, had three or fewer staff members. In the smaller libraries there was seldom a staff member who was not involved in public service, and who might be able to work outside the building without affecting that service. Even in the larger libraries in the project, it was unusual to have a single staff member who worked exclusively in technical service functions.

If guest libraries sometimes had problems freeing staff, hosts sometimes had problems accommodating them. Many host libraries operated in buildings which were over-crowded, so that providing space for the terminal and printer presented difficulties. In two cases the only available location was the director's office. Accommodating a guest required that a work area around the terminal be kept relatively clear. In crowded conditions, this was sometimes difficult.

Other environmental factors that affected cluster arrangements were traveling distances, lack of public transportation outside downtown Peoria, and the problems of traveling in the winter. In addition, the IVLS system area is served by a number of telephone companies. It is not unusual for a phone call covering less than five miles to involve long distance charges. This, and the necessity of going through an operator to charge calls, made communication between the host and guest libraries an annoying procedure. The poor quality of phone connections in some areas hindered the use of dial access terminals.

Three basic alternatives were available for cataloging work in the clusters: (1) a guest library staff member took books or order slips to the host library and ordered cards; (2) a guest library staff member took order slips to the host library before the book was received and made printouts. Upon receipt, the printouts were edited and batched so a staff member could return to the terminal to order cards and make printouts for new orders; or (3) the host library did catalog card editing and ordering for the guest based on order slips or other information. Incorrect cards were re-ordered. Interlibrary loan work was handled four different ways: (1) the host monitored the guest request file, informed them of any pending requests and took care of all updating; the guest did not use OCLC to borrow items; (2) the host took care of lending operations and borrowing operations for the guest; (3) staff members from the guest library went to the host library to handle lending and borrowing transactions on the terminal; and (4) guest libraries shared a dial-access terminal to process ILL transactions. Of the two general cluster arrangements: having guest staff members travel to the host terminal or having host staff members perform the routines for the guest—the first alternative worked better in the project.

Clusters with libraries of the same size and clusters with libraries of varying sizes provided different but valuable advantages for their members. In the former, staff members understood each other's needs and priorities. There was also a belief that the terminal belonged jointly to equal partners even though it was housed in one library. In the latter, where the hosts were large libraries and the guests were much smaller, the host often believed that by housing the terminal and making it available, they were helping smaller libraries to experience the advantages of automation. Librarians from the smaller units of service felt they improved their relations with the larger library staff and that they benefited from the greater experience and expertise of that staff. In both cases, the cooperation and cohesiveness of libraries serving the same area improved; neither of these host-guest configurations, in itself, affected the success of the cluster.

Both clusters which mixed library types and those whose members were the same type also had advantages for their members. Where all the cluster members were of one type, visits to the host library were an opportunity to exchange ideas on mutual concerns. Multitype clusters, however, promoted understanding among library staff with different but often complementary interests. Although clustering allowed some use of OCLC by guest libraries, the librarians in the project strongly preferred, and were generally willing to pay for, full in-house access. Clustering provided an effective, low-risk way to introduce OCLC to libraries but seemed to lead to a desire for full use rather than to satisfaction with clustering as a long-term arrangement. In particular, using a terminal for interlibrary loan was very difficult in a guest situation. As a result, some participants believed that if they could not afford to have a terminal in-house, belonging to OCLC might not be worth the cost.

## PUBLIC ACCESS TERMINALS

One measure of the success of public terminals was the effect they had on interlibrary loan requests initiated by the libraries during and after terminal availability. With the exception of the largest public library, all types showed substantial increase in ILL activity, particularly in the middle of the public access period. In nearly all cases, the growth in ILL activity was sustained after the public terminal was removed. In some cases, the ILL rate a year later was even greater than it had been with the public terminal present.

Guest libraries, compared to host libraries, experienced a greater and more immediate increase in ILL activity during the public access period. Host libraries, on the other hand sustained the increase more consistently after the public terminal left. The major public use related advantage mentioned by all libraries was the enthusiasm of the public and their increased awareness of and understanding of the interlibrary loan process. There was a definite public relations benefit. The major disadvantages of public terminals perceived by the staff were: (1) the staff time needed to supervise or instruct; (2) the tendency for children to play with them; and (3) down time.

As a result of public terminals, patrons generally became more aware of the power of their libraries to serve their needs. The perception of the library, in most cases, was extended to include its role in a resource sharing network, primarily as a borrower, but sometimes as a lender as well. This increased awareness was evident not only in patron comments and staff observations, but also in the inter library loan statistics for the participating libraries. Despite its advantages, however, a public access terminal is an expense few libraries the size of those studied could afford. Such libraries, however, benefited from placing a work terminal in a public area or otherwise allowing partial public access to it.

## CATALOGING

During the project, the costs of cataloging on OCLC were closely examined. The costs of cataloging before OCLC were more difficult to determine, but an effort was made to approximate pre-OCLC conditions and calculate estimates.

The libraries in the project had three principal sources for cataloging cards before OCLC: Vendor cards ordered with some or all of their purchases; typing complete card sets in-house; and using a card duplicating or mini-master machine with a typed stencil for the unit card. A summary of costs in terms of time and money for each procedure is given in Table III.

The figures for various libraries were compared to each other both within the same cataloging method and among methods. These comparisons did not produce any meaningful correlation of cost or time with staff size, population served, budget, acquisition rate or collection size. One factor, however, did correlate well with the time needed to catalog. This was the amount of information provided on the catalog cards.

The amount of information given depended on the training of the librarian or the staff members and what they believed was necessary for their patrons. This variation did not seem to depend upon the size of the library or the background of the staff per se, but rather on the emphasis placed on the cataloging function. Some librarians reported that a good deal of the information generally found on catalog cards was misleading or confusing to patrons, while others reported that they should follow national standards as much as possible.

*OCLC Cataloging—Content.* The introduction of OCLC influenced the cataloging process beyond merely changing procedures. Staff members that had been typing their own catalog cards were now presented with more data than they had before. The availability of additional information often made them more conscious of its value for themselves and their patrons. Libraries that had been using vendor cards did not necessarily receive more data with OCLC, but often they could manipulate and customize it more easily.

TABLE III

PRE-OCLC CATALOGING

|  | In-house Typing | Vendor Cards | In-house Reproduction |
|---|---|---|---|
| **Minutes per title** |  |  |  |
| Range | 21.87 - 4.75 | 9.41 - 1.16 | 28.85 - 5.71 |
| Median | 8.94 | 5.06 | 13.28 |
| Mean | 9.84 | 4.86 | 16.06 |
| **Cost per title** |  |  |  |
| Range | $3.868 - $.451 | $1.580 - $.703 | $5.189 - $.717 |
| Median | $.693 | $.982 | $2.740 |
| Mean | $.912 | $1.046 | $2.750 |

Five librarians, however, expressed the opinion that there was more information on the OCLC record than they needed. This, they felt, was confusing to staff and, with public access terminals, to patrons. In a few libraries enough information was deleted from the OCLC record that the resulting card sets were very similar in content to the pre-OCLC cards.

In one area, however, the OCLC cataloging process could not always meet the needs of the public libraries in the project. The staff of these libraries were very conscious of the need to move books from the processing area to the patron area as quickly as possible. They found that the seven-day delay in receiving cards was a distinct disadvantage.

*OCLC Cataloging—Time and Cost.* A detailed worklog study was done of OCLC terminal operations and related activities. Terminal operations were measured for cataloging, retrospective conversion, interlibrary loan and miscellaneous activities. Table IV summarizes the results of the cataloging worklog study.

The total sample depicted was 3,991 operations, which are listed according to the frequency of their use. As Is refers to limited editing, often no more than changing the local holding code and call number. Modified means more extensive editing. In Referred Operations cataloging records were not produced, they were referred to another staff member via a printout or save file.

If these values are weighted by their percentages and added together, an average number of minutes per title can be estimated. The weighting of the time needed by the percentage of occurrence for an operation provided an overall average of 3.129 minutes per title. A second worklog sheet was kept to measure OCLC-related activities which took place away from the terminal, such as preparations for cataloging, processing cards, etc. Tabulations in this case are shown in Table V.

The need for activities both at the terminal and away from it varied widely from library to library depending on their cataloging procedures and whether they were host or guest. In general terms, academic, special, school and large public libraries tended to need more time per title for OCLC cataloging, whereas smaller public libraries tended to need less.

*Comparison of OCLC and Pre-OCLC Cataloging.* Any comparison of the project data for pre-OCLC and OCLC costs is tentative, because, except in four cases, the data were not gathered in a very reliable manner. Data on OCLC cataloging times should be

TABLE IV

OCLC CATALOGING
Summary of General Operations

| Operation | Time in Minutes | Percentage of Sample |
|---|---|---|
| Modified | 3.088 | 54.0 |
| As Is | 1.275 | 23.4 |
| Referred | 1.734 | 19.7 |
| Not Found | 1.572 | 2.0 |
| New Input | 12.307 | 0.9 |

TABLE V

OCLC CATALOGING AND RETROSPECTIVE CONVERSION
Activites Away from the Terminal

| Activity | Minutes | Units in Sample |
|---|---|---|
| Cataloging preparation | 2.925/title | 2,458 |
| Checking OCLC Cards | .234/card | 8,744 |
| Book Processing | 2.902/title | 2,705 |
| Host/Guest Phone Calls | 3.024/call | 106 |
| Travel Time (Guest Libraries) | 13.774/trip | 42 |
| Retrospective Conversion Prep. | .776/title | 1,512 |

more accurate because of the care taken with the study, the large amount of data gathered, and the decreased degree of control the workers had on the outcome. In all comparisons, it must be kept in mind that the pre-OCLC cataloging data probably underestimates time and costs.

Most, if not all of the libraries studied saved time through the use of OCLC for cataloging. Even the travel time for guest libraries, if pro-rated on a per title basis, did not offset the gains in most cases. In general, greater time savings were realized by smaller public libraries which averaged 6.38 minutes per title. Larger public libraries gained much less, averaging only .88 minutes per title.

The introduction of OCLC also affected the level of staff needed for cataloging operations. The larger public libraries that did not report large savings in terms of salary costs or minutes per title did, however, shift work to staff members at lower pay levels. Presumably, libraries with more staff members or with greater variation in staff pay levels could take advantage of the opportunity to shift the work load. In the smaller libraries with a limited number of staff members, this was not possible. Indeed, in these smaller libraries either the same staff member did the work in both OCLC and pre-OCLC cataloging or the work was shifted upward in the hierarchy.

From the studies, it seems that most libraries benefited from the implementation of OCLC either by using less staff time, using less expensive staff time, and/or by freeing more highly qualified staff for other activities. However, although the payoff of OCLC use may be staff time, the cost is in the unit charges and terminal maintenance expenses.

For all public libraries in the project, it is likely that OCLC cost them more overall than pre-OCLC cataloging. The smaller public libraries, serving a population of less than 5,000, had an estimated average added cost of $1.95 per item. The larger public libraries, serving a population of 5,000 plus, estimated average cost increases per title of $2.06—not a great deal more than for the smaller libraries.

*Benefits of OCLC Use for Cataloging.* Most libraries reported increasing the number of access points to their collections through OCLC use. A comparison of the in-house cataloging done for the pre-OCLC test and for OCLC cataloging later in the project showed that there were an average of 6.4 percent more added entries and 67.2 percent more subject entries on the OCLC cataloging. There was also a strong perception by 88 percent of the directors, expressed in the project interviews, that the quality of cataloging had improved. This meant more information on the cards for staff and patron use, a fuller record which included contents and summaries. Using OCLC also made the cards more consistent in the choice and form of entry.

We had expected the complexity of the OCLC record to be a negative factor, but it was not. When asked, at the end of the project about the display format, 10 directors said it was very clear and 12 said that it was fairly understandable. No director felt that working on the terminal was too complicated. Moreover, using the shared cataloging database, occasionally contributing to it, and having the opportunity to loan materials to other libraries gave many staff members a feeling of being in touch with the larger library community.

Despite higher cataloging costs, OCLC was retained by most of the project libraries because of other benefits. The access to resources in the libraries was improved because OCLC cataloging encouraged the use of more subject headings and added entries. The quality of cataloging generally improved, offering more information for patrons and staff. In some cases, OCLC provided faster turnaround on cataloging cards, but this was by no means universal. Finally, most libraries valued OCLC chiefly for its resource sharing capabilities. The high costs of cataloging was seen as the price to be paid for increased access to resources.

## *INTERLIBRARY LOAN*

Before the project began, almost all the system libraries got their interlibrary loan requests filled by sending paper forms to the Illinois Valley Library System. There various methods were used to obtain the material, in accordance with a statewide set of protocols. By the end of the project participating libraries were filling many of their own requests over OCLC using locally adapted protocols; the data base of location holdings had more than doubled; a new statewide delivery system was introduced; and other changes had taken place.

One of the most spectacular results of the project, which may have affected interlibrary loan patterns and costs, was the growing number of local library holdings symbols in the data base. In June, 1979 there were 221,000 such holdings symbols, most contributed by three academic libraries. By the end of 1983 there were 738,000. More than half were contributed by project libraries, which meant a high proportion of holdings symbols from public libraries.

*Online Interlibrary Loan—Borrowing.* In order to measure the library staff time needed for interlibrary loan after the use of the OCLC subsystem began, a library worklog study was undertaken in the Fall of 1981, after libraries had time to gain some facility in the new procedures. Each library was asked to record, for four weeks, time spent at the terminal for all types of OCLC work and time spent away from the terminal doing OCLC-related work.

An analysis of interlibrary loan records for borrowing operations for 945 new requests searched, where 624 were online requests, showed that finding an item in the database took an average of 2.79 minutes. Finding it and sending a request took about 5.63 minutes.

Thus, once an item was located on the database, the actual request initiation—filling out and producing the online ILL form—took 2.84 minutes. The search itself appeared to take less time—2.36 minutes rather than 2.79—if it was not successful.

Initiating the request, of course, automatically involved the library in later updating operations on the terminal; this was also studied. The average time for a borrower-related activity other than request initiation was 1.75 minutes at a cost of $.165. For each of the 625 new requests initiated on OCLC during the study, there were 1.81 borrower-related updates. When 1.81 updates per request was taken as an average, the staff cost of the updating activity was approximately $.30 per OCLC request initiated. Table VI compares ILL borrowing costs to the libraries and the system.

All labor costs were based on 1980 salary levels plus 11 percent for benefits. All OCLC costs were based on 1981 charges for OCLC use. The total staff costs for lending-related terminal operations was estimated for this group of libraries on the assumption that the balance of operations found in the worklog study was typical. Taking the yes answer as the base, i.e., everytime a library could it sent the item requested, a library received 2.09 pending requests for each one answered yes. For every yes answer there were .67 no answers, .07 conditional answers and .36 future date answers given. Also, for every item lent, or yes answer, there was an average of 3.39 other times the library accessed the ILL files related to lending activities, i.e., to check the pending file, update records or check on

TABLE VI

**INTERLIBRARY LOAN BORROWING COSTS**
Comparison of ILL Methods Studied

| Method | Cost to Library Per Request | Cost to System Per Request | Total Cost Per Request | Library Staff Time Per Request |
|---|---|---|---|---|
| Paper request to IVLS, no online activity at library | $1.36 | $3.35 | $4.71 | 15.18 min. |
| Online request sent by library | $3.62 | — | $3.62 | 17.48 min. |
| Online search by library, paper request sent to System | $2.07 | $3.35 | $5.42 | 14.90 min. |
| Online search by library, request by telephone | $2.18 | — | $2.18 | 15.37 min. |

record status. The total terminal-related staff time for these various lending operations was 8.44 minutes at a cost of $.46. When non-terminal activities, i.e., retrieving the item, shipping, etc., were included, the cost was $1.53. This cost multiplied by the number of items lent approximates the cost to project libraries for operations related to online lending. If the request was received on an ALA form, the cost was approximately $.91 as opposed to $1.53 for requests received online. The cost to process a telephone request was approximately $.90, excluding postage and mailing supplies for out-of-state fills.

In general, the total use of interlibrary loan by all IVLS libraries increased over the period of the project. From 1980 through 1983, except for two quarters, the total interlibrary loans in the system increased every quarter over the same period the previous year. Recorded interlibrary loans included paper requests made by phone from library to library. The interlibrary loan requests made by libraries can be broken out in two ways—paper requests versus OCLC requests, and requests from OCLC libraries regardless of communications medium versus those from non-OCLC libraries. Table VII charts these figures.

The table shows annual totals for ILL requests initiated by the 72 IVLS libraries. Paper requests are those sent on forms to IVLS headquarters and processed there. OCLC libraries include all project participants plus two other OCLC libraries that did not participate in the project, but sent requests online. Pre-project OCLC libraries in-

TABLE VII

INTERLIBRARY LOAN REQUESTS IN ILLINOIS VALLEY LIBRARY SYSTEM

|  | 1980 | 1981 | 1982 | 1983 |
|---|---|---|---|---|
| All ILL Requests Sent | 24,717 | 25,630 | 30,037 | 32,819 |
| **PAPER REQUESTS** | | | | |
| From OCLC Libraries | 16,993 | 10,187 | 11,021 | 13,720 |
| From non-OCLC Libraries | 2,363 | 3,252 | 4,372 | 4,408 |
| All Libraries | 19,356 | 13,439 | 15,393 | 18,128 |
| **OCLC REQUESTS** | | | | |
| Pre-Project OCLC Libraries | 4,694 | 4,592 | 5,224 | 6,885 |
| Project Libraries | 667 | 7,599 | 9,420 | 7,598 |
| All OCLC Libraries | 5,361 | 12,191 | 14,644 | 14,483 |
| **REQUESTS FROM OCLC LIBRARIES** | | | | |
| Paper requests | 16,993 | 10,187 | 11,021 | 13,720 |
| OCLC requests | 5,361 | 12,191 | 14,644 | 14,483 |
| All requests from OCLC libraries | 22,354 | 22,378 | 25,665 | 28,203 |

clude these two plus four project partial participants—three academic libraries and one public. Project libraries are the full participants. Some of these used OCLC ILL before training in 1981, because staff already knew the subsystem from earlier jobs. OCLC requests sent from system headquarters were not counted, since they were the result of paper requests from libraries.

In 1981 most of the OCLC project participants began using the ILL subsystem, yet that change in methods did not seem to effect their total ILL use. Although the number of recorded requests they generated remained virtually the same, the method shifted from paper to online.

There are two possible, but unverifiable, explanations for these apparently stable interlibrary loan rates. The first is that after identifying local holdings over OCLC, libraries may have secured the material via a telephone call rather than an online or paper request. The second is that the libraries took advantage of reciprocal borrowing. This policy, shared by all IVLS members, insured that cards from one library would be honored by all others. Patrons of OCLC libraries, when informed that a title was held by another nearby library, may have gone there rather than use ILL services. Statistics from IVLS indicate that there was a large increase in reciprocal borrowing during the latter half of 1981 and the beginning of 1982.

From 1981 to 1982 the number of ILL requests in the system grew by 4,407, an increase of 17.2 percent. Despite the cessation of project support in mid-1982, 75 percent of this increase came from OCLC libraries, and 75 percent of these additional 3,287 requests, or 2,453 requests, were sent online—a 20 percent increase over the previous year. Paper requests also grew eight percent during 1982 for OCLC libraries and 34 percent for non-OCLC libraries. Total transactions during 1983 generated in the IVLS area, increased 9.3 percent over 1982's 2,782 requests. Virtually all of this growth came from OCLC libraries which had a 9.9 percent increase in interlibrary loans.

One of the premises of the project was that inputting a large number of local holdings symbols to a shared data base would increase the number of requests filled locally. This did not occur for requests processed by IVLS headquarters. First, the overall fill rate for paper requests did not show any definite change from 1978 through 1982. Second, the fills from IVLS libraries did not clearly increase over the time of the project. If anything, fills from Reference and Resource Centers, Illinois libraries, and out-of-state libraries, showed a gradual increase. On the other hand, ILL requests handled directly by OCLC libraries had a 94.7 percent fill rate. In practice, the OCLC users filled as many requests as possible through OCLC—preferring local sources. Additional requests that were more difficult or that required inordinate amounts of staff time were sent to system headquarters. Thus, the IVLS ILL department was maintaining its fill rate despite a change in the nature of the requests received.

*Response Time.* In-house online access to local holdings and the ILL subsystem greatly improved turnaround time on requests. A transaction study showed that in late 1980, the average turnaround time experienced by libraries was 16.2 days. A sampling of IVLS paper requests over four and one-half years confirmed this figure. In the slowest requests, OCLC decreased turnaround by two to three weeks. Seventy-five percent of the requests sent online were generally filled within two weeks.

*Patterns of Activity.* During the project studies, we were especially interested in the effect that adding large numbers of public library holdings symbols to the database would have on borrowing patterns among types of libraries. Because most of the libraries in the project were public and the overwhelming majority of the ILL requests sampled came from these libraries, we could make some assessment of borrowing patterns. The data we studied showed that public libraries received a much higher percentage of their materials from other public libraries when requests were filled within IVLS. When their requests went out of the IVLS area, the percent filled by academic libraries went up.

In addition to the nature of the material requested, a possible explanation is the distribution of OCLC libraries by type within IVLS. Twenty-two of the 35 OCLC libraries were public libraries and half the local holdings symbols belonged to public libraries. In Illinois, outside of IVLS, the proportion of public libraries to other types using OCLC was smaller, while in the nation as a whole, public libraries accounted for only a small percentage of all OCLC members. When a request could be filled within IVLS, public sources were available and used extensively. Outside IVLS they were less available and, consequently, less used. Thus, contrary to some libraries' fears, if more public libraries were to join OCLC, it is likely that the burden of their ILL requests would fall more on other public than on academic libraries.

Because of the large number of public libraries of varying sizes involved in the project, it was also possible to study the lending patterns among them on the basis of size. The results showed that the single large public library obtained as much from its neighboring small libraries as from the major state public library. Of all the public library sources used by this large library, the local medium size public libraries supplied the most.

Medium size public libraries, serving populations of 5,000-50,000, filled the majority of their requests from other public libraries and chiefly from medium size ones. However, almost three times as many requests were filled for them by small public libraries as by the Peoria Public and almost none were filled by the Chicago Public. The same pattern appears even more strongly from small public libraries.

This pattern is not the result of relative numbers of holding symbols on the OCLC data base. By the end of the project, the large public library had contributed 29.8 percent of IVLS public library holdings symbols on OCLC, yet it filled only four percent of the public library requests. Medium size public libraries contributed 55.5 percent of the holdings symbols and filled 81.3 percent of the requests. Small public libraries contributed 14.7 percent of the holdings and filled 14.7 percent of the requests.

The patterns of borrowing indicate that:

1. Larger public libraries fill most of their patrons' needs for material typically held by public libraries from their own resources, and use ILL mostly for obtaining materials from academic libraries.
2. Large public libraries are not a good source for public library ILL requests. Although they have large and varied collections, they also have large local demand and cannot make popular materials available to other libraries.
3. Medium size public libraries serve as the major resource for materials to public libraries of all sizes. The smaller the borrowing library, the more likely it is that their needs will be met by a medium size library.
4. Small public libraries have more to offer to each other and to medium size public libraries than do large libraries in terms of the numbers of ILL requests that can be filled from their collections. One reason for this may be that popular books acquired in smaller libraries may not have many local readers, so they are soon free to fill other libraries' needs.

Most of the material borrowed online from IVLS libraries was requested by IVLS libraries. The percentage, however, got generally lower over the 17 months of the study as a higher percentage of requests were filled for other libraries in Illinois and, to some extent, out-of-state libraries. One class of borrowers outside IVLS accounted for a large percentage of the loans. This was the headquarters of the other 16 Illinois library systems who mediated requests for their own libraries. Of the 180 items in the study lent by IVLS libraries to Illinois libraries, 147, or 81.7 percent were sent through other systems.

In a few cases, the systems which borrowed from IVLS libraries used OCLC to catalog materials for their public libraries, thus adding their holdings to the database for resource sharing. However, most libraries that borrowed through systems did not contribute information about their holdings to the database. The lack of online information about these holdings has created a situation of one way access. It has already been demonstrated that public libraries do have resources that are valuable to other public libraries, no matter how small they are (Altman,1970; Markuson, 1977; Turock, 1981). Libraries need to explore ways to promote access to these holdings for mutual resource sharing.

*ILL Use and Staff Attitudes.* The transfer of responsibility and control of interlibrary loan transactions from the system headquarters to the IVLS libraries and the wider role these libraries played as borrowers and lenders was a major factor in their reactions to OCLC use. In interviews with library directors at the end of the project, they cited increased patron access to resources as the chief benefit of OCLC in their libraries. Resource sharing was the main reason most libraries kept on using OCLC after the project, according to both directors and governing authorities.

The most valued aspect of interlibrary loan was simply access to resources—being able to verify and locate items patrons needed. Although the speed of ILL services increased with online transactions, only nine of the 29 directors felt this was of great importance. Seven directors said specifically that confirmation of availability—regardless of the time needed to obtain an item—was important for their patrons' satisfaction.

Over 70 percent of the directors believed that online service produced a change that patrons noticed. The facets patrons commented on were the increased speed, access to information or resources, and a perceived higher likelihood that the material would be what they wanted. These patron reactions resulted in higher use of ILL, good will for the libraries and an enhanced image of library service and the people who provided it.

## COST OF OCLC

The major disadvantage of the use of OCLC for most libraries was the cost. There were at least three separate aspects of the cost factor which concerned the directors and boards. The first was the absolute cost, that is, whether or not the amount of money needed to support OCLC was available or could be obtained now and on an ongoing basis.

The second facet was present in at least half of the libraries. This was a concern not with the amount of money involved per se. The directors were concerned with how they could justify the amount of money needed to their board, and the boards were concerned, in many cases, with how to justify the expenditure to their communities.

A third facet, openly expressed by several librarians, was related to the intangible aspects of automation. There was some distrust of technology, not so much for itself, but for the difficulty it presents to the uninitiated in understanding its operations and assessing its value. There was also considerable uneasiness about price changes for OCLC services and for telecommunications. All of these factors together added up to a general sense that it was impossible to prove clearly one way or the other that a specific type of automation was doing its job, that it was the best product to do the job, and that the job it was doing was necessary.

## THE DECISION

Interviews were conducted with directors, board members and staff members to determine what general factors influenced the decision to keep or drop OCLC at the project's conclusion. These included:

1. *Evaluation data and strategies*. The project provided librarians and their boards with evaluation data and strategies. It was considered unusual to have such a clearly defined decision-making framework and to have available such a complete package of information.

2. *Initial decision.* An important factor in the eventual decision a library made at the end of the project was the decision they thought they would make when they began the project.
3. *Proliferation of computers.* The general social-technological mood in the country played a role in determining whether libraries would continue with OCLC. As one librarian expressed it, her board was in a "computer mode"; they were ready to accept technology and computers as a legitimate means of improving service.
4. *Role of the library.* The image that the director and the board had of the library and of itself was another important factor. If the library was perceived in more traditional terms, it was less likely that the board would decide to continue with OCLC.
5. *Public awareness.* Public awareness of the library was equally important. In some towns, the library was perceived as a city showcase, a major institution in the community which reflected its concern for education and modernization. The public access terminal and the good public relations that it supplied enhanced this view of the library both in the eyes of its board and in the eyes of the citizens at large.
6. *Library size.* The smaller the library, the more holistic and philosophical the librarian and the board were in seeking and evaluating OCLC benefits.
7. *Role of bibliographic control.* A library was more likely to continue with OCLC if there was a clear and conscious understanding of the link between uniformity in cataloging and resource sharing.
8. *View of staff.* Directors were more likely to perceive that staff time was being better used when the library was large enough to have several full-time employees. In smaller libraries where there were only one or two employees, there was less likelihood that directors would perceive staff as separate from themselves. It was more likely directors would note increased staff satisfaction but not necessarily perceive increased staff efficiency.
9. *Long-range planning.* The libraries that had developed a long-range plan were more clearly able to define the basis of their decisions and to justify them to their governing authority through reference to that plan. Directors were somewhat more comfortable with their decision and less likely to doubt that they had made the right choice.

## CONCLUSIONS

From measurements undertaken during the project the following general conclusions were drawn concerning OCLC use by the project libraries:

1. Anticipated problems with OCLC, and with any automation, include anxiety about coping with technology, and learning new skills—either for oneself or for other staff. Implementation need not present these problems. For OCLC, at least, implementation presented instead unanticipated problems of down time, response time and documentation. In some cases, confidence in oneself or others' abilities was lower than necessary and expectations of perfection from the computer or OCLC staff were higher than might be reasonable.
2. OCLC's cataloging subsystem was appreciated more for improved quality of cataloging than for improved efficiency, although the latter was noted in most cases. Almost all directors acknowledged this enhanced cataloging information and most felt it was a benefit both to staff and patrons. Cataloging, however, was not an important benefit to governing authorities.
3. Resource sharing on OCLC became increasingly important as the project progressed. Although it added to staff workload in most cases, it was viewed as the prime benefit of OCLC, particularly by governing authorities. It was, in some cases, appreciated both for extending the resources a library could offer its patrons and for extending the use made of the library's own collection. Access to additional resources was generally valued more than speed in acquiring those resources.
4. Increased staff effectiveness and efficiency was an OCLC benefit that was not always realized quickly. About 18 to 24 months were needed to adjust procedures and train staff so increased efficiency could be developed. In some cases, where pre-OCLC procedures were particularly efficient, this benefit might not be realized. It was as likely that staff time would be used more productively as that it would be saved.
5. OCLC use served to improve the public and/or staff image of the library, but this benefit did not last for a long period. The introduction of this new library tool provoked attention for a while, but it soon became an accepted and expected part of library services.

6. The costs of OCLC use, the justification of those expenses, and insecurity about future costs increases were the chief barriers that had to be overcome by project libraries in making a decision to continue OCLC use.
7. The availability of a local source of information, training and assistance was a strong factor in the libraries' positive reaction to OCLC. Most of the directors of the libraries that retained OCLC felt that this kind of help should continue to be available.

The introduction of OCLC to a large number of public libraries in one region had many effects on their service, and on regional cooperation. Some of these are reported in this article. The clearest proof of the benefits to the libraries was the large number that retained OCLC at the project's completion. The clearest proof that cost was an inhibitor was the number that could not continue, even though that was what they wished to do.

## REFERENCES

Altman, Ellen. "The Research Capacity of Public Secondary School Libraries to Support Interlibrary Loan." Unpublished PhD Dissertation, Rutgers University, Graduate School of Library and Information Studies, New Brunswick, New Jersey, 1970.

Bills, Linda G. *Cataloging Before and After OCLC*, Illinois Valley Library System: OCLC Experimental Project Report. Springfield, Illinois: Illinois State Library, June 1983.

Bills, Linda G. *Implementing OCLC in Small and Medium-sized Libraries*, Illinois Valley Library System: OCLC Experimental Project Report. Springfield, Illinois: Illinois State Library, November 1982.

Bills, Linda G. *OCLC Experimental Project Description*, Illinois Valley Library System: OCLC Experimental Project Report. Springfield, Illinois: Illinois State Library, October 1982.

Bills, Linda G. *OCLC Public Access Terminals in Small and Medium-Sized Libraries*, Illinois Valley System: OCLC Experimental Project Report. Springfield, Illinois: Illinois State Library, July 1984.

Bills, Linda G. *OCLC Use by Library Clusters*, Illinois Valley System: OCLC Experimental Project Report. Springfield, Illinois: Illinois State Library, May 1983.

Markinson, Barbara. *Analysis of Requirements of On-Line Network Cataloging Services for Small Academic, Public, School and Other Libraries: A Demonstration Project Using the OCLC System. Final Report*. Bethesda, MD.: ERIC document Reproduction Service, 1977. ED 140 861.

Turock, Betty J. "Performance, Organization and Attitude: Factors in Multitype Library Networking." PhD Dissertation, Rutgers University Graduate School of Library and Information Studies, New Brunswick, New Jersey, 1981.

# The Kewanee Public Library Votes Yes on OCLC

Harriet Conklin

Probably the Kewanee Public Library would never have considered joining a bibliographic network in late 1979, except that it was proposed by the Illinois Valley Library System (IVLS) of which the library is a member. The Kewanee Public Library has a service area of two townships with a population of about 16,000, and both an urban and a rural constituency. At present the Library is open 61 hours per week, has a collection of about 50,000 titles, a staff of 8.5 FTE's and a budget under $200,000. Kewanee is relatively remote from any large metropolitan area, being 50 miles from both Peoria and the Quad Cities. Despite its isolation the Board of Trustees has prided itself over the years on keeping the Kewanee Public Library in the mainstream of library development. Founded in 1875, the Library has consistently taxed at the maximum allowed by law, has developed a substantial endowment fund which more than covers the materials budget, and has maintained, in good condition, the handsome Carnegie building which was constructed in 1908. However, the city has not grown over the years; in fact the last few decades have seen the population decline and library income level off. Of great benefit to the Kewanee Public Library was the establishment in 1965 of the state-wide network of 18 Cooperative Library Systems.

## *JOINING THE EXPERIMENT*

When it was proposed by the Director of the IVLS that Kewanee join the IVLS/OCLC Experimental Project and it was further explained that the equipment and ongoing costs would be covered by the project for three years, there was little hesitation on the part of

---

Harriet Conklin, Director, Kewanee Public Library, Kewanee, IL 61443.

© 1986 by The Haworth Press, Inc. All rights reserved.

the library board in agreeing to be a participant. The library staff was equally enthusiastic at the prospect of seeing the library move toward automation.

While the board and staff were eager to have the library become a member of the OCLC network and they looked forward to learning how to use the online system effectively, there was no one on the staff who had any knowledge of OCLC or of computers in general. Without the guidance of the IVLS consultants our participation in the project would have been impossible. From the perspective of the staff, acceptance of the IVLS/OCLC Experimental Project was never a factor. After the initial introduction a few members avoided the computer, but most were anxious to use it, particularly for searching. Nor was age necessarily an indication of interest. Presently the only staff member who is doing any original cataloging is not a professional librarian; she is also the oldest member of the staff.

Over the years the Kewanee Public Library has found it difficult to recruit and retain a professional staff. There are several possible reasons for this problem among which are location, size, and budget. The great advantage we saw to the OCLC cataloging subsystem was that it allowed quality, individualized cataloging to be produced by a non-professional staff. The only original cataloging which has been done at the Library since becoming a member of OCLC has been of local history items, local area publications, recently released LP recordings, and cassette tapes. Otherwise we find cataloging on OCLC for all the items we add to our collection regardless of the source from which they have been received. Certainly the ability to edit the cataloging to our own specifications is an added plus. For us that editing is primarily a matter of deletion.

## *RECON AND ILL*

Upon becoming a member of the OCLC system first priority was given to retrospective conversion. Training for this task was not difficult and most of the RECON project was carried out by volunteers—two very loyal board members—and high school student pages. Initially all items with copyright dates of 1975 and forward were entered into the database. Later all local history items and adult nonfiction copyrighted before 1975 were also added. At this time the Kewanee Public Library has no specific plans for an online catalog or an automated circulation system. However, with the retrospective conversion of the majority of the collection an accomplished fact, implementation of either option would be easier.

The other function of OCLC which the Library has used to date is the Interlibrary Library Loan subsystem. The advantages are obvious—the ability to borrow materials not owned by our small library to meet the needs of the community and to reciprocate by loaning to other libraries from our collection. Even a library as small as ours does have some unique items. One title is held by only 11 libraries nationwide, according to the OCLC record. The Kewanee Public's copy has been shipped 17 times in the past three years, primarily out of state, to fill ILL requests.

The interlibrary loan service is highly valued by the community. Again nonprofessional staff have been able to learn quickly and easily to carry out this service. The use of the OCLC terminal is of benefit in searching for acquisitions as well. During the IVLS/OCLC Experimental Project we learned to use the OCLC printer to generate book order slips by deleting most of the information on the screen leaving only what is needed for the book order. A print-out of the pertinent information is made onto a two part order form which is then sent off to the book jobber. This has turned out to be a simple, cost effective way to use the OCLC database.

## *OCLC STAYS IN KEWANEE*

The time of decision was at the end of the project late in 1982, when it became necessary to commit local funds, if we were to continue to be a member of the OCLC bibliographic network. As a demonstration project the IVLS/OCLC experiment was a success as far as our library was concerned. The consensus of the staff was that we must keep the membership. This view was presented to the library board who agreed, approved the cost, and signed a contract with the Illinois State Library to continue membership. The contract is reviewed annually.

## *CLUSTER FAILS*

One aspect of the IVLS/OCLC experiment which we hoped might have an impact on lowering our costs was setting up a cluster arrangement in which the Library acted as a host, housing the OCLC terminal and having various neighboring libraries use it on a guest basis. At one time or another during the project we had six guests, all located within a radius of 20 miles. A weekly schedule was set up assigning time for a staff person from each of these libraries to use the terminal for retrospective conversion, cataloging, and ILL. The Kewanee Public also checked the ILL file for each of the guests once or twice a week, depending on the frequency of their use.

At the time the project ended it was hoped that the guest libraries would help support the fixed costs of maintaining the terminal, prorated by the time they actually used it. However, only two of the six libraries chose to remain with OCLC and of these only one chose to cluster. For a full explanation of clustering, its implications and results, Linda Bill's 1983 project report presents the details. Since the clustering concept did not work out, the full burden of paying the OCLC costs had to be assumed by our library. Any cost savings that could be made were followed. All cataloging was done in non-prime to take advantage of lower rates. Catalog cards were produced only one day a week to cut down on postage charges.

Through ILLINET it is relatively easy to project the OCLC charges for the coming year. Since the Illinois State Library allows a discount for prepayment, we take advantage of the discount and the savings. The costs have been fairly constant over the past three years. The reasons include the fact that the number of items to be cataloged is declining, the Illinois State Library has subsidized costs somewhat for libraries of our size, and interlibrary loan activity has remained relatively constant. In fact, this past year ended with a surplus in the OCLC account.

## *THE NEGATIVE SIDE OF MEMBERSHIP*

Two negative aspects associated with the use of the OCLC system for libraries of similar size and location should be noted. The first is the high telecommunications charges resulting from having to maintain a dedicated telephone line. In a metropolitan area where low cost long distance rates are available, dial up access to OCLC is the logical answer to cutting expenses. Maintaining a dedicated line is very costly and only partially compensated for by lower wages and living costs in this rural area. At the moment we have no choice but to stay with the dedicated line; if there were a cheaper alternative, however, we would surely use it.

The second negative aspect is that OCLC did not develop the automated circulation subsystem that was projected several years ago. The experiment participants had expected that it would tie in directly with the project. It would have been a logical continuation of the IVLS project and an option that the Kewanee Public had hoped would become available.

If it were necessary to answer the question of whether joining the OCLC bibliographic network lived up to the majority of the expectations that existed at the time the decision to join the experiment was made, the answer would be a clear affirmative. Having available the resources of the OCLC bibliographic network has proved to be extremely valuable to the Library as we strive to maintain quality service with both limited personnel and financial resources.

## REFERENCES

Bills, Linda G. *OCLC Use by Library Clusters, Illinois Valley Library System: OCLC Experimental Project Report*. Springfield, Illinois: Illinois State Library, May 1983.

# We'll Wait and See

Thomas H. Ballard

My charge from the PLA Task Force on Network Relations is to tell you something about Plainfield, New Jersey, its library, our attitudes towards participation in bibliographic networks, and the reasons for our position. Financial considerations, New Jersey's network, Union County's efforts, and the role of the public library are also part of the picture. In other words, our decisions concerning automation are interwoven with most of the other major decisions required to determine how best to serve Plainfield; they are often in conflict with the prevailing expectations of other libraries in New Jersey.

Plainfield has chosen to ignore cooperative types of automation entirely and yet invest heavily in microcomputers. Therefore, we have declined to join the OCLC network (even when the first year costs would have been paid by our State Library); we don't intend to participate in a cooperatively owned CLSI circulation system presently in the planning stage (although the county government is expected to fund the hardware costs); and we have no plans to purchase access to DIALOG, SDC, BLS, and other similar utilities. Yet we are not against automation. We own a minicomputer-based cataloging system, MINI-MARC, and have 12 work stations with upper-end microcomputers, expansion disk drives, and assorted hard drives. The rest of this paper will seek to explain our situation and our reasons for these automation decisions.

## THE PLAINFIELD PUBLIC LIBRARY

Plainfield is a study in contrasts. Through the 1920s many of the local residents boarded their private railroad cars for the trip into New York each morning. In the evening they returned to their great Victorian houses. Plainfield's prosperity survived the Depression,

---

Thomas H. Ballard, Director, Plainfield Public Library, Plainfield, NJ 07060.

© 1986 by The Haworth Press, Inc. All rights reserved.

although it was considerably reduced. Now Plainfield is a minority community. The great houses are multifamily dwellings, 60 percent of the population is black, and other minority groups are growing in size. Plainfield's library is heavily impacted by these changes in the community as might be expected. Its once large circulation has dwindled to three per capita, but it is financially sound, perhaps rich, with a large endowment and several Winslow Homer original paintings. Its collection is unusual for a town of 45,000—130,000 titles and 175,000 volumes in a 46,000 square foot modern building.

Perhaps the most salient characteristic of the Plainfield Public Library is its status as an Area Reference Center in New Jersey— one of 26, which receive substantial state funding for the provision of backup reference help, ILL clearance, delivery services, etc. This monetary aid usually amounts to about $70,000 per annum, or approximately 10 percent of Plainfield's income. This year, however, New Jersey traded in its old system of cooperation and opted for multitype networking. The new legislation creates six regional groupings of all types of libraries; no one library is guaranteed financial support any longer. Now each region will contract for services within its boundaries and Plainfield will soon lose any guarantee of financial aid from this source. As we shall see, this has been an influential factor in our automation decisions.

## *THE UNION COUNTY AND NEW JERSEY SITUATION*

The main thrust of the State Library has been to win passage of the new networking legislation, a goal achieved in 1984. The second objective, as I understand it, was to prepare for statewide, multitype networking. To accomplish this, a single direction was chosen for endorsement—namely OCLC. Although applications were required for the substantial funds set aside for the purpose, it's fairly certain that any Area Library that would join OCLC through PALINET would be subsidized for all costs during the first year. Many of the Area Libraries took advantage of the offer with the result that the incidence of OCLC membership in New Jersey has expanded considerably during the past several years. The ultimate goal of multitype resource sharing is dogma at the State Library of New Jersey with no consideration of alternatives and no substantial opposition from the librarians in the State itself. New Jersey can be said to be fully committed to the resource sharing paradigm at this time.

The situation in Union County is also one with a networking emphasis. To set the scene, Plainfield is located on the far western border of the county and yet is only 30 miles from New York City. Union County is, therefore, small in size (102.68 sq. mi.) and very densely populated (504,094 population). Many of the municipalities in it are quite prosperous and one drives between them with almost no indication that political borders have been crossed. Within the borders of Union County are three of the present 26 Area Libraries and several others with collections above or nearly 100,000 volumes. There are also some very small public libraries, a county community college, and numerous special libraries of some distinction (Bell Laboratories, for example).

With a small, densely populated geographic area and an above average level of economic prosperity, Union County would, therefore, seem to be well-situated for resource sharing activities. The first step in this direction began in 1984 with a feasibility study for a cooperatively owned circulation system for the twenty public libraries, one school library, and the community college. The report from the consultant recommended a CLSI system at a central location. With the findings of a unique title study in hand, the plan would be to convert the collections of a few towns using Carrollton's REMARC service and then convert the rest of the towns from the resulting database. There are also expectations that the county government would be willing to invest in the required hardware and/or retrospective conversion costs. The motivation of the librarians favoring this approach seems to be primarily an interest in obtaining an automated circulation system, but for some the interest in resource sharing ranks nearly as high.

As indicated, Union County's three Area Libraries will soon disappear into the Union-Middlesex Region, one of the six regions created under the new networking legislation. This future event has led to some changes in present cooperative practices. Several informal, reciprocal borrowing agreements have been disbanded and steps taken to incorporate all the public libraries and others that might want to join under a single organization called Libraries of Union County Consortium (LUCC), which will represent Union County's interests within the region and serve as a vehicle for the receipt and disbursement of any County funds that might be received for automation projects.

In summary, then, there is a great deal of networking activity in Plainfield's environment at present. The librarian activists have been involved in the establishment of the Union-Middlesex Region and others have been more involved than usual. Indeed, the prospect of an automated circulation system, public access catalogs, and computer-generated management information reports is eagerly awaited. Progress is a word on everyone's lips in local professional meetings.

## *PLAINFIELD'S POSITION*

Plainfield is having a difficult time in this environment. On the one hand it seeks to be a good neighbor and on the other it does not believe in the direction of present activities. Without the faith, Plainfield finds itself unable to accept the costs that arise from the networking emphasis in the state.

The basis for Plainfield's objections is economic—public libraries exist in a world of choices. When resources are devoted to one activity, they cannot be used for anything else. Therefore, it's reasonable to look at two types of costs instead of one: (1) how much an activity costs, and (2) the relative effectiveness of this activity versus the benefits estimated to arise from diverting these resources to the best alternative activity. In my opinion, and based on limited evidence which is nonetheless more than that presented by resource sharing enthusiasts, a larger book collection available for browsing is a much superior alternative to costly networking.

## *CIRCULATION AND INTERLIBRARY LOAN*

I have questioned the value of resource sharing in earlier articles (Ballard, 1982 and 1985). Table I contains the information supplied to me in a 1984 survey of the contribution of interlibrary loans to public library circulation in the states and in the Canadian provinces that were able and willing to provide the data. Nine states and one province, including Arkansas, Connecticut, Vermont, Iowa, Georgia, Massachusetts, Wyoming, Colorado, Kentucky, and Newfoundland indicated that they had no data on this activity.

To better understand the data shown, bear in mind that:

1. The Alaska figures are for requests rather than for loans and were adjusted according to an overall fill rate of slightly more than 88 percent. They are, therefore, incorrect to the extent that the public library fill rate differs from that of the entire state.

2. Data from Michigan are derived from four semi-annual ILL reports and there are problems. The reports take samples of two weeks in March and October and multiply by 26. In my experience, these are unusually busy months and multiplying by 26 may cause large errors. The figures are for requests. I have assumed a fill rate of 90 percent and the sample includes from 63 to 67 percent of public libraries in the four reports. Therefore, results are adjusted upwards to compensate. I probably would not have included these data except that it's certain that Michigan does not fit the normal pattern shown by the other states. Suspect as they are, the Michigan data are needed as compensation for the other reports.
3. Minnesota's figures include reference questions.
4. Actual ILLs in the Prince Edward Island libraries were only 500, but the libraries are all part of a single system. Internal, or intralibrary loans, are estimated to be more than 7,000 based on 5,807 requests often filled with more than a single book.
5. The Rhode Island ILL figure is for requests rather than filled ILLs.
6. The North Dakota state circulation is taken from the *ALA Directory* and is for FY1981, while the ILLs are for FY1983. Therefore, the percentage of circulation may vary upward or downward depending on the change in circulation.

The results for 32 states with some sort of usable data fall within a very narrow range and are probably, in all cases, less than two percent of total public library circulation. For the U.S. libraries only, total circulation was 843,821,572 and interlibrary loans were 4,804,787 or 0.57 percent of total circulation. In Canada there were 956,559 ILLs from a total of 124,243,139 or 0.77 percent of total circulation. The combined U.S. and Canadian circulation was 968,064,711 with 5,761,346 ILLs, or 0.60 percent of total circulation. The recently released National Center for Education Statistics data confirm the general impression about the relative magnitude of ILLs as found by my survey. It reported that during 1982, public libraries received 4.8 million ILLs while circulating 1,113.2 million items. ILLs were, therefore, 0.43 percent of total circulation (Heintze, 1985). Reciprocal borrowing, while more effective, is nonetheless small as well. Table II contains some figures on reciprocal borrowing as a percentage of circulation. More comprehensive data are hard to locate.

It remains only to say that Plainfield also conforms to the pattern

## TABLE 1

### INTERLIBRARY LOANS AS A PERCENTAGE OF PUBLIC LIBRARY CIRCULATION

| STATE | TOTAL CIRCULATION | TOTAL ILLS | ILL % OF CIRC | YEAR |
|---|---|---|---|---|
| AL | 12,139,142 | 49,661 | 0.41 | FY1983 |
| AK[a] | 2,136,490 | 13,293 | 0.62 | FY1983 |
| CA | 111,000,000 | 228,682 | 0.2 | FY1979 |
| DE | 2,185,094 | 14,996 | 0.69 | FY1984 |
| FL | 35,906,395 | 62,794 | 0.17 | FY1982 |
| IL | 59,005,559 | 525,833 | 0.89 | FY1984 |
| ID | 4,900,000 | 25,000 | 0.51 | FY1983 |
| IN | 31,496,122 | 67,042 | 0.21 | FY1983 |
| KS | 11,893,466 | 73,220 | 0.62 | 1983 |
| LA | 13,678,102 | 77,896 | 0.57 | FY1983 |
| ME | 5,705,869 | 45,000 | 0.78 | FY1983 |
| MD[b] | 32,164,132 | 154,930 | 0.48 | FY1983 |
| MI | 36,552,785 | 833,403 | 2.28 | FY1982 |
| MN[c] | 28,688,687 | 631,533 | 2.20 | FY198? |
| MS | 7,134,008 | 26,140 | 0.37 | FY1983 |
| MO | 25,510,569 | 57,000 | 0.22 | Latest |
| NV | 3,847,611 | 9,048 | 0.24 | FY1983 |
| NH | 5,486,403 | 13,167 | 0.24 | FY1982 |
| NJ | 33,269,520 | 141,674 | 0.43 | 1984 |
| NY | 87,147,714 | 1,008,214 | 1.16 | 1982 |
| NC | 25,064,293 | 76,380 | 0.305 | FY1983 |
| ND[d] | 2,813,767 | 11,571 | 0.41 | FY1983 |
| OH | 78,117,285 | 107,980 | 0.14 | 1983 |
| OK | 10,405,709 | 32,459 | 0.31 | FY1983 |
| PA | 38,632,329 | 206,219 | 0.53 | 1982 |
| RI[e] | 4,424,630 | 35,647 | 0.81 | 1983 |
| SC | 9,636,352 | 16,464 | 0.17 | FY1983 |
| TN | 14,432,375 | 59,294 | 0.41 | FY1983 |
| TX | 44,775,379 | 106,410 | 0.24 | FY1983 |
| UT | 10,446,200 | 7,680 | 0.074 | 1983 |
| VA | 30,942,000 | 26,402 | 0.085 | FY1983 |
| WA | 25,191,032 | 59,755 | 0.24 | 1983 |
| Alberta | 15,438,226 | 37,115 | 0.24 | 1982 |
| Brit. C. | 26,128,397 | 188,610 | 0.72 | 1983 |
| Manitoba | 4,794,617 | 9,123 | 0.19 | 1982 |
| New Brun | 2,765,073 | 2,994 | 0.11 | FY1983 |
| Nova S. | 4,301,393 | 10,243 | 0.24 | 1983 |
| Ontario | 62,588,872 | 305,378 | 0.49 | 1982 |
| P.E.I. | 575,000 | 7,500 | 1.30 | FY1984 |
| Saskat. | 7,651,561 | 395,596 | 5.17 | 1983 |

observed in Tables I and II. This library's patrons received 247 interlibrary loans in 1983. Its reciprocal borrowing from other neighboring libraries amounted to a total of 3,726 items during the same year (while loaning 9,379). Plainfield's circulation in 1983 was 131,511. Considering this data from the standpoint of Plainfield residents, it's necessary to subtract the reciprocal loans to outsiders from total circulation and add back books loaned at other libraries. When this is done, ILLs are nearly 0.2 percent of total circulation to Plainfield residents and reciprocal loans to them are 2.96 percent of total circulation. In other words, nearly 97 percent of all lending to the Plainfield community occurs from the locally owned collection.

## OCLC AND PLAINFIELD

There would seem to be two primary reasons for wanting to be a part of the OCLC system—OCLC as a source of quality cataloging and OCLC as an aid to resource sharing. In our analysis of the wisdom of participating, we carefully kept the two functions separate and the discussion will maintain this separation.

Plainfield, as an Area Library, is obligated to purchase a minimum of 5,000 titles each year; our normal level of acquisitions is usually between five and six thousand with the latter figure more likely. But Plainfield has no branches and, therefore, it's uncommon for us to acquire multiple copies of any given title. We noted that the OCLC first time use (FTU) charge of $1.46 was a serious problem to us. In an issue of *Library Technology Reports* we also discovered that telecommunications charges per terminal from Minnesota were approximately $200 per month (Matthews and Williams, 1982). New Jersey is farther from OCLC than Minnesota, but we would

TABLE II

A COMPARISON OF INTERLIBRARY LOANS AND RECIPROCAL BORROWING AS A PERCENTAGE OF PUBLIC LIBRARY CIRCULATION

| LOCATION | RECIP LOANS | % | ILLS | % | RECIP/ILL |
|---|---|---|---|---|---|
| Essex County, NJ (1984) | 70,000 | 1.63 | 7,000 | 0.16 | 10.00 |
| Union County, NJ (1983) | 70,060 | 2.81 | 7,200 | 0.29 | 9.73 |
| Illinois (avg.lib. 1981) | 3,580 | 3.95 | 737 | 0.81 | 4.86 |
| N. Suburban (1983)[1] | 886,559 | 8.1 | 31,048 | 0.28 | 28.55 |
| Illinois Valley (1983)[1] | 185,036 | 7.04 | 19,558 | 0.74 | 9.46 |
| Indiana (1983) | 509,801 | 1.62 | 67,042 | 0.21 | 7.6 |
| New Jersey (1984) | 1,133,370 | 3.41 | 141,674 | 0.43 | 8.0 |
| British Columbia (1983) | 670,000 | 2.56 | 188,610 | 0.72 | 3.55 |
| Burr Oak (1982)[1] | 138,200 | 6.16 | 21,593 | 0.96 | 6.4 |

[1] One of the eighteen library systems in Illinois.

also be joining the system through PALINET, the regional broker in this area. We were not particularly concerned about the cost of terminals which are a one-time figure in the budget, but factoring in the maintenance charges for storing records, tape preparation, card sets, etc., it didn't seem wise to investigate the matter any further. We abandoned the idea completely and began to look for alternatives.

At this point in 1981, we were concerned with the possibility of acquiring an automated circulation system in the future. We realized that retrospective conversion would be required at some point and part of our considerable interest in OCLC was that this process would get underway. Therefore, the fact that machine-readable records would be generated in the cataloging process was important to us. The alternative to OCLC that attracted us was the MINI-MARC system from Informatics, now LSSI. For the cost of $52,000 we were able to acquire a stand-alone minicomputer cataloging system with the entire MARC database on 1,500 or 1,600 inch floppy disks. This system is configured by the company to match the library's particular requirements, it utilizes the full MARC format, and its highly sophisticated printer produces a quality card set and spine labels at great speed. Furthermore, the record that is printed is also written to a user floppy disk, so catalog conversion is underway with MINI-MARC as well.

As a cataloging tool, MINI-MARC is probably the equal of OCLC in many respects and often better. While a ROM reader was formerly required to determine which of the 2,100 floppy disks had the desired record and whether it was on side A or B, present practice saves this step by calling the record from laser disk drives. It can then be edited as desired in much the same way as OCLC. The final product is a card set and a machine-readable cataloging record. For cataloging purposes, its disadvantage is that only MARC records are in the database, not the other millions of user records. Like most public libraries, however, we seldom purchase books that are not in the MARC database and we also find over 70 percent of our retrospective holdings as well. MINI-MARC also has advantages. There is no response time problem and the system is definitely faster than OCLC for this reason. Off-hour usage makes no difference—MINI-MARC can be used whenever it's convenient for the operator and without financial penalty. Another great advantage has been the ability to let less skilled operators create the machine readable records and have them reviewed and revised by our cataloger before they are printed. Finally, the card sets are not mailed but printed each day. Interfaces with automated circulation systems also exist for our future.

Weighing the advantages and disadvantages of MINI-MARC and OCLC is very much a matter of the type of library and its collections. If Plainfield were a research library, the existence of the additional millions of user records might make OCLC the better choice but for cataloging in a meduim-size public library, we feel that MINI-MARC is a superior system to provide our needed cataloging while converting our records to machine-readable form.

Cataloging, however, is only one of the functions of OCLC. It may not even be the principal one. The great advantage of OCLC is that thousands of libraries are inputting their records into its database and a member library can determine almost immediately who owns a book wanted by a patron but unavailable in its own collection. Through the ILL subsystem, OCLC will pass the request electronically to one library, then another, and then to a third. This will be done automatically and instantaneously. Plainfield's MINI-MARC system has no such capability. The advantage of OCLC in this respect is undisputed but the magnitude of that advantage needs some consideration. Just how much is this capability worth?

From Plainfield's standpoint, one must consider the alternatives available to us as well as the OCLC advantages. New Jersey has three levels in its system hierarchy and Plainfield is at the second level. When an ILL request is received, we decide whether it's likely to be owned in any of the 18 member libraries in our Area and then send the request around to the others if this seems appropriate. Because the other libraries are smaller than Plainfield, they would be unlikely to have OCLC even if we did. In other words, the fact that Plainfield had OCLC would have nothing to do with our knowledge of the holdings of the other libraries, nor the ability of our member libraries to know the holdings of Plainfield. If the local option fails, we know about it in three or four days and can then call the Newark Public Library (which has OCLC) for locations. A few days are lost. There is also a very good chance that Newark will be able to fill the request because it has an extensive collection. When one analyzes the time required for ILLs, it's not the U.S. mail but rather the speed with which the lending library processes an item that is the major cause of delay. OCLC has very little to offer in this respect. The OCLC subsystem often means that the time from a request to its delivery to a patron is 11 days rather than 15, or 20 days rather than 24. Either way, this type of access is acceptable to very few patrons—a fraction of one percent.

## *PRESENT AND FUTURE COST COMPARISONS*

No decision about MINI-MARC or OCLC should be made without comparing the costs of the two systems. For this purpose the following assumptions were made. First, Plainfield would have to join PALINET in order to gain access to OCLC. Next we assumed that we would utilize the system to catalog 6,000 new books and 6,000 already owned each year. We assumed a cost of capital of 10 percent and we decided that our ILLs would rise from 247 to 500 and that we would use the OCLC ILL subsystem, the serials check-in subsystem, but not the acquisitions subsystem. We feel justified in comparing OCLC including subsystem costs with MINI-MARC which does not have these capabilities on the basis that anyone buying a clock/radio rather than a clock would obviously use the radio.

Given these assumptions, the annual cost to Plainfield to be, a member of OCLC and PALINET is roughly $30,000. Capital costs for terminals and site preparation have been ignored completely as incidental. Because the billing factors are so many and so complicated, the accuracy of this estimate might be off 10 percent in either direction, but the figure is conservative rather than lavish. The cost of MINI-MARC varies greatly under different scenarios. To begin with, however, the system costs $52,000 to purchase. For this sum we received a ROM reader, the minicomputer itself, the entire MARC database on floppy disks, and a $5,000 printer. If we had not bought the system, it's assumed that we would have received $5,200 as a return on capital. After the first year, there was a maintenance contract charge of $620 per month and an additional cost of $385 per month for floppy disk updates to the MARC database. Taken together, MINI-MARC cost us $17,260 during the second year of operation. This was the "going first-class scenario".

By the end of the second year we had discovered that breakdowns are not common and decided to drop the maintenance contract altogether. We estimated that a service visit would cost approximately $1,000 or more because we would have to pay air travel costs, per diem, $85 per hour, etc. Nonetheless, at $620 per month, it seemed worth going without the contract. With all of these possibilities, and perhaps with luck as well, our maintenance costs for the third year were under $2,000, making the cost of operations only $11,800 for this period. Please note that this includes the assumed $5,200 that would have been received in interest on our capital. Our actual cash outflow was only $6,600. This might be called the "self-insured scenario".

Now consider the "disaster scenario" should it ever occur—the City of Plainfield decides that the Library is not nearly as important as additional social programs and fails to increase our budget. Perhaps the State decides that it must be less generous. Hovering in the background of our thinking was the precarious nature of our funding as an Area Library. What would happen if Plainfield's budget came under serious pressure? If we had OCLC, we would have no choice but to sit down and write out the $30,000 check, offset somewhat by the $5,200 earned from capital. But in the MINI-MARC "disaster scenario", we could stop purchasing floppy disk updates, concentrate on retrospective conversion with the existing database, and use MINI-MARC as the excellent cataloging-word processor that it is. Our total out-of-pocket expense to operate the system becomes something like $2,000 for maintenance and probably much less than this. In other words, OCLC costs are in some sense fixed costs, but the MINI-MARC costs can bend with the times. Given the savings that we have achieved over the OCLC option for these three years, we could, in fact afford to purchase an entire backup MINI-MARC system at this time and still be $15,000 ahead (the second system costs $35,000 because there is no need to acquire a second database).

## *OTHER MORE SPECULATIVE CONSIDERATIONS*

OCLC has pointed with pride to the fairly stable FTU costs to users noting that they increased only 17 percent during a period in which the Producer Price Index rose at a much faster rate (*LJ/SLJ Hotline*, 1983). In another article, I speculated about why this might have been the case (Ballard, 1983). It seemed to me that much of this could be accounted for by the fact that the OCLC system was growing rapidly during the period. The revenues received from each additional member in a highly capital-intensive service environment were considerably more than the additional costs of serving the newcomer. All previous members of OCLC were, therefore, the recipients of benefits from the expansion of the whole system even though they might complain bitterly about response time. The pace of growth during these years cannot possibly be sustained, however.

The question to ask is what will happen to OCLC's costs when growth in the system stops entirely? I continue to believe that as this occurs, the costs of the OCLC system to its users will rise more rapidly than they have in the past. Yet a more serious situation would arise if alternatives became available that would actually lead present members to leave OCLC. If, for example, a microcomputer became available that would perform the functions presently available through MINI-MARC at a cost of $10,000 to $15,000, the barriers to purchase would be greatly reduced. In a declining membership environment, OCLC costs would most likely rise more rapidly than the Producer Price Index. Events have overtaken this 1983 speculation with the availability of BiblioFile at a minimum cost of approximately $7,000 for computer, software, laser disk, and printer. The level of sales of this system and its impact upon OCLC membership should be closely followed.

The other major problem now facing OCLC and its membership is the breakup of the Bell System with its accompanying deregulation of prices. It seems likely that communications costs are going to rise very sharply in the near future—something like a 25 percent increase is considered an optimistic prognostication. The slowdown in growth was an inevitable cause of price increases, but significant rises in communications costs will only exacerbate an already cloudy future. If these unexpected expenses are sufficiently serious, they will serve to hasten the time when growth in membership will cease to occur. OCLC will try to lessen the damage as best it can and is moving in this direction. It has announced a major capital expenditure for new computer equipment designed primarily to reduce the impact of communication cost increases. To what extent this will be possible and at what cost to the membership is impossible to predict at this time.

Another speculation concerns the copyrighting of the OCLC database. Why has this been done? OCLC claims that this action was taken in order to stop abuses and to protect the membership. It's also possible, however, that OCLC has looked at its future prospects and decided that a large measure of institutional self-protection may be needed. It's certainly this possibility that has the state librarians worried. If the database cannot be freely used within the states to create networking, then most of their emphasis on OCLC was misplaced. The possibility exists for OCLC to demand fee payments from networking activities in the future, if OCLC records are used to create regional databases. In the case of records created solely from public domain MARC records, regional networking cannot be restricted in any way.

## IS PLAINFIELD A GOOD NEIGHBOR?

As the largest collection in its region, Plainfield would indeed be depriving the other libraries if they were OCLC members but Plainfield were not. In this case, they would be unable to go to their terminals and determine whether or not Plainfield owned a title. Such is not the case in the Plainfield Area or elsewhere when the Area Library has joined the OCLC system. The smaller libraries cannot justify the expense of OCLC membership and do not join when the Area Library does so. The importance of OCLC or MINI-MARC to the smaller libraries is that the Area Library is undergoing conversion of its records. As this process proceeds, the possibility of a fiche catalog or a CD-ROM disk of the larger library's holdings becomes more and more possible for purchase by the other libraries. The fact that retrospective conversion is accomplished by MINI-MARC or BiblioFile rather than OCLC may be an advantage depending upon what OCLC does with its copyright claims.

Plainfield is perfectly willing to donate its cataloging records to any state database at any time and has the right to do so. If the State Library wants to take our records and tape load them into OCLC, it's free to do so and this can be done for less than the cost of supporting our membership in OCLC for a single year. Indeed, it's a bargain for the State Library. Were this done, the state network would know what Plainfield's holdings were and could request them at will. Only Plainfield is supposedly disadvantaged, because we would not know what everyone else owns. Plainfield's partial rejection of the network is a cause of no injury to other libraries in New Jersey.

## RESOURCE SHARING

Who is hurt by our decision? Not the other libraries and not Plainfield either. The figures on our present level of ILL borrowing were given earlier. Plainfield borrowed 247 books in 1983 which was 0.2 percent of total circulation. Our cost estimates for OCLC membership assumed that this might rise to 500 if we joined the system. In other words, we don't anticipate that knowing what the other libraries in the nation own would be of great benefit to us. Mentioned earlier also was the Union County CLSI system proposed by a consultant. Much of the enthusiasm for the jointly owned automated circulation system arises from the ability that it would provide for any library to determine not only whether another Union County library owned a book, but also whether or not it happens to be on the shelf at the moment it's wanted. The problem with this system is that it would have annual costs to Plainfield of approximately $10,000. We doubt very much that there would be an increase in either ILLs or reciprocal borrowing that would justify this kind of expense. We will be glad to donate our machine-readable cataloging to this system as well, however.

We have two reasons for rejecting the resource sharing paradigm. The first is that it's so little used at the present time. From this data we believe that there is a kind of fundamental patron behavior at work. Patrons want to browse among books. They must be able to see a book, pick it up and look at it, and only then do they consider borrowing it. The assumption made by the resource sharing paradigm is that people can be tantalized by bibliographic records as well as by books themselves. We doubt it very much. Plainfield has a significant part of its collection in limited access stacks with bibliographic control of these holdings in the same catalog with the open-shelf books. The closed stack books are little used in comparison to the rest of the collection—probably because it precludes browsing. Indeed, it's fortunate that this is so for our delivery system would completely collapse if they were in demand equally with the self-service parts of our collection. We can foresee no possible combination of future technology that can possibly improve on the accessibility of a closed stack collection. Online catalogs coupled with telefacsimile equipment cannot improve upon it.

Our second reason for rejecting resource sharing is that its effectiveness is assumed but not demonstrated. There are a number of co-operatively owned circulation systems in existence in the U.S., but who has ever seen "before and after" figures about the levels of resource sharing? When state libraries seek to create state multitype networks, who has ever heard them predict the level of resource sharing as a percentage of total circulation that will result from the new system? Resource sharing is a very peripheral activity and it's justified only if its expense is also small. Thus far the networking plans in the Plainfield environment don't meet this test. They are instead very expensive.

## *CONCLUSION*

Plainfield's attitude toward the bibliographic utilities is summarized in the title of this article, "We'll Wait and See". The choice of MINI-MARC over OCLC is logical and cost effective, if only cataloging is at issue. If resource sharing in the future becomes orders of magnitude larger than at present, then Plainfield will be well placed to change its present strategy. Through MINI-MARC, we will have created our retrospective machine-readable cataloging records. We can tape load our records, sign the papers, and order our OCLC terminal. If this does not take place, we are still in a good position. We continue to create the machine-readable records while awaiting the availability of a microcomputer circulation system of sufficient power to handle a collection of our size. It's just around the corner. But if the resource sharing paradigm fails as we expect, then the networking leadership is in trouble. Well, perhaps not—it's unlikely that anyone will ever trouble themselves to document the failure. It's like that with dogma.

## REFERENCES

Ballard, Thomas H. "Dogma Clouds the Facts", *American Libraries* 16 (April, 1985), pp. 257-59.
_____. "Library Systems: A Concept That Has Failed Us," *Wilson Library Bulletin* 60 (December, 1985). pp. 19-22.
_____."Why I Don't Want to Join OCLC," *Unabashed Librarian* 47 (1983), p. 4.
Ballard, Tom. "Public Library Networking: Neat, Plausible and Wrong," *Library Journal* 107 (April 1, 1982), pp. 679-83.
Heintze, Robert A. "A Survey of Public Libraries 1982," *Public Libraries* 24 (Summer, 1985), p. 59.
*LJ/SLJ Hotline* 12 (May 30, 1983), p. 4.
Matthews, Joseph H. and Williams, Joan Frye. "The Bibliographic Utilities: Progress and Problems," *Library Technology Reports* 18 (November/December, 1982), p. 634.

# A WLN Dilemma

Mark A. Nesse

Everett, Washington is a small Puget Sound community of 56,800 located 35 miles north of Seattle. Everett's public library was founded in 1894 and consists of a main facility, a bookmobile, and a small branch. The vital statistics—as of January, 1985—were: 26 FTE staff; 102,300 titles; 142,000 volumes; plus 80,000 U.S. documents, since the library is a partial depository. The 1985 budget totaled $1,046,512 with books at $208,750 and the 1984 circulation at 600,375. EPL is governed by a five member Board of Trustees.

## INITIATING A BIBLIOGRAPHIC NETWORK IN WASHINGTON

Washington State and the Pacific Northwest have been leaders in the resource sharing movement for many years. The Pacific Northwest Bibliographic Center (PNBC) was founded in 1940, and served as an ILL switching center for libraries from Oregon, Washington, Alaska, British Columbia, Idaho, and Western Montana through the union catalog it maintained at the University of Washington. As such monster filing systems go, this was a good one. Member libraries sent a unit card for each new acquisition, and unlike at least one similar effort, sent a card when an item was lost or withdrawn so that the PNBC catalog would be corrected.

Thus it was not surprising that when MARC tapes began to flow from the Library of Congress, Washington was one of the first states to recognize the potential. In 1969, the Washington Library Network was formed with LSCA Title III funds. Planners envisioned a database built primarily on LC-MARC, with member contributed cataloging for items not available through LC. The software was written by Boeing Computer Services for mainframe hardware

---

Mark A. Nesse, Director, Everett Public Library, Everett, WA 98201.

(IBM/AMDAHL) located at Washington State University. WLN was able to learn from OCLC's problems, and the software was built around a series of indexed files, including an authority file, since many member libraries were creating subject and name entries for a common database. Each new record was also reviewed by WLN staff for errors.

The first online participants of the Washington Library Network were seven regional/county public libraries. All of these libraries had been created following enabling legislation passed by the Washington Legislature in 1948. They tended to have a good deal in common: Few had system-wide catalogs in their branches, their collections were light in older materials, most operated libraries in small to medium size towns. The need for union catalog information was far greater than the need for circulation control, and none was blessed or cursed with a central/main library and its attendant problems. The ability to get good cataloging products, such as spine labels, cards and pockets, and generate system-wide fiche catalogs of their holdings was very useful. The holdings information for ILL fits their needs and service philosophy. However, as other libraries with different needs began to consider joining WLN, pressure grew for other services.

## *ADDING SERVICES*

In the mid-seventies WLN began to talk about developing an acquisition module and a circulation module. After the usual round of task forces and committee meetings, it was decided that Tacoma Public would function as a pilot. They would develop a circulation system that met both its requirements, and WLN's requirements. Furthermore, Tacoma's system would be mini-based, and an interface with the WLN bibliographic system would be developed. Never dreaming that the term interface could mean different things to different parties, Everett's naive expectation was that such a circulation system would be debugged by Tacoma, and then made available to other WLN members for a pittance.

Tacoma signed a contract with Data Phase in 1977, and began its adventure with automation. Everett Public had funding to join WLN in 1977, but decided to wait for two reasons: (1) the Tacoma/WLN circulation module seemed distant, and (2) we were worried about future funding. The prospect of conversion to an automated system, closing the catalog, and then having the funding cut out of some future budget caused considerable concern. Discussion among our staff members centered on whether we should join WLN, or whether we should try to find the additional money for a circulation system and build a database on the fly. The final decision was to wait, since it seemed safe. In the meantime, in an effort to learn from Tacoma's experience, we started a substantial weeding project.

Neither of the above reasons for hesitation was resolved in 1978, but we received a clear message that our funding for automation would not be carried forward into another budget year. Reports in the library press were uniformly optimistic about the WLN project's future (Franklin and MacDonald, 1976). So in late 1978 Everett Public came to be a fully fledged online participant in the Washington Library Network, and began to learn the wonders of network costs: For example, the cost of adding one copy of two new titles = 2 × $1.60, or $3.20; the cost of adding two copies of one new title = 1 × $1.60 + $.05 or $1.65.

## RECON, CATALOGING AND THE NETWORK

Up to this time most of the attention of WLN member libraries had been focused on adapting their current cataloging programs to the network environment. However, being keenly interested in the circulation module, Everett was one of the first libraries to raise questions about retrospective conversion. WLN finally made a policy decision that online retrospective conversion would be virtually free. From the network's perspective, this resulted in a wider, deeper database which would both aid marketing the network and enhance resource sharing among member libraries. From Everett's perspective, it was too good to be true.

Before plunging ahead with retrospective conversion, we pondered whether to add everything in the shelf-list, or whether to conduct an inventory and add only confirmed holdings. Conventional wisdom at that time suggested that we enter the entire shelf-list, and then delete holdings from the database for those items that turned out to be missing when bar code labeling was finally done for circulation. However, from sampling that had been done earlier, we estimated that over 10 percent of the collection was probably missing, and that it was fair to assume that these missing titles were in demand. As a result, we conducted an inventory from the shelf-list, and in the process wrote the LC card number that was printed in the book on the shelf-list card. Some of the missing items were reordered.

After a six month lapse of time to catch the stragglers coming back from circulation, we began WLN's free online retrospective conversion from the shelf-list, in most cases using the LC card number and adding our local call number to the WLN database. When it was announced that the RECON program was going to be terminated, we stepped up our input until we had two terminals going 12 hours per day. Free online retrospective conversion was replaced by a minimal charge batch program. Using this version, we continued to chip away at the project until the spring of 1982.

Meanwhile, we had decided that if the network database was to function as our local catalog, and if the network was to provide our cataloging, we would cover our network costs by functioning without a cataloger. When the head of technical services left, we did not fill the vacant position. Instead we created a clerical supervisory position to manage the day-to-day operation of the department and realigned Technical Services to report to the coordinator of Administrative Services. The latter also managed circulation, budget, and personnel. In taking this move, we made two explicit points: (1) automation should not add substantial overhead to the library's operation, and (2) books should pause in technical services only briefly on their way to the shelves and not be lost to delays over bibliographic hair-splitting.

While discussing how such an arrangement would function, an early question came up, "Without a cataloger, what will we do about buying new books that aren't in the database?" We decided not to buy them, because:

1. Our hit rate for new acquisitions on WLN was close to 98 percent. Since we were adding about 4,000 titles per year, this meant we would either have to do without approximately two percent of that number (80 titles) or buy titles on the same subject that were in the database.
2. We believed the public would prefer that we spend our limited resources on books rather than on a part time cataloger to catalog these 80 titles per year.
3. Since in a community of 56,000, local publishing is virtually non-existent, we were not in danger of missing a local history gem.

The next question dealt with who would decide which WLN catalog cards we would file during the time that we were maintaining a card catalog and adding holdings to the database. Like most libraries, our cataloger had always filed some cards, modified some, and had thrown some of LC's handiwork in the trash can. The answer—we would file them all. Reason: Like it or not, they were all being stored on our behalf in the network's computer. Reaction to this arrangement was mixed. Some colleagues regarded it as genius; some felt it was symptomatic of intellectual decline. In fact, some of our staff became afflicted with classic symptoms of network avoidance syndrome. There was much ado made about WLN's clean database and no one wanted to be the butt of snickering at the next Washington Library Association conference over some cataloging fine point.

## THE COM CATALOG

When we began to plan for our first COM catalog, we asked other WLN members for advice. All had opted for fiche, and nearly all were using the entire WLN holdings file. In other words, each set included several hundred fiche, and holdings for a given library were interfiled among all other WLN member holdings. The reasons for this choice had been primarily financial: Fiche readers are cheaper than 16mm readers (such as Information Design or Autographics models), and a copy of the entire database fiche set was cheaper than the cost of generating a custom catalog of only a given library's holdings. Most directors said they were pleased with this system. Heretofore many of them had functioned without any kind of union catalog in the branches. However, when we talked with librarians, all agreed that, while fiche was better than nothing, it was very confusing for patrons. Fiche were misfiled, a bother to use for the public, and frequently patrons tried to locate an item that actually belonged to some other library system. As a result, Everett opted for COM that contained only local holdings, and chose 16mm film which was mounted on Information Design ROM III readers. The cost for microfilm only for the 37,000 titles converted up to that point was $1,600.

We finally concluded that it was impossible to continue maintenance of the card catalog amid the inventory project and the RECON project, and we closed the card catalog in 1981. This resulted in a situation where staff had to check four places to determine whether or not we had a given book: (1) the card catalog for older materials that had not been located in the database, (2) the COM film catalog for things that were in the database, (3) a biweekly microfiche update, and (4) an on-order card file.

## ONLINE CIRCULATION AND INTEGRATED SYSTEMS

While we worried about conversion, the catalog, and the public's long-suffering reaction to both, our first concern was still the circulation system. There had ensued what seemed like an interminable series of meetings among Data Phase, the Tacoma Public and the Washington State Library, on behalf of the Washington Library Network, intended to move plans forward for a circulation system. By mid-1981, however, we had given up on the WLN possibility, and found that a number of vendors, besides Data Phase and CLSI, had emerged. Furthermore, most of the systems were moving in the direction of an integrated approach to library automation. It was becoming apparent that a vendor who provided only a circulation system simply wasn't going to be a real competitor in the marketplace. Authority control, the beginnings of acquisitions systems, black box interfaces with networks, and Public Access Catalogs in varying degrees of sophistication were available from different vendors.

We had neither the time nor the money to keep a circulation system, a bibliographic network, and a manual acquisitions system in sync with each other. Since the major book vendors maintained full MARC databases, they seemed like logical possibilities for reasonably priced records. However, when we inquired, all tried to sell us their acquisitions system. Bro-Dart and Blackwell declined, explaining that they would prefer to wait for an industry standard to which they would provide an interface. This was reasonable. Baker and Taylor declined because they felt such a move would undercut marketing efforts of their own acquisitions system, which seemed to us a poor reason. Baker and Taylor was trying to corner some form of vertical market, and seemed unfazed by our statement that whoever provided an interface and MARC records would also get our book business.

In our search for an affordable MARC record, we discovered MINI-MARC, a floppy disk based system for retrieving MARC records which could then be used for the production of cards. Unfortunately, having converted to COM, we were not in the market for cards. Science Press and Information Design, who made our microfilm readers, were possibilities, but both were expensive, especially their cost to sort our database for new COM cumulations. As part of our investigative librarianship, we had learned that there are three basic costs in COM catalogs: (1) the MARC records; (2) a computer run to sort the database into author/title/subject sequence, and spool this data onto magnetic tape in print-ready format; and (3) the cost of producing a master and copies in the desired microformat from the print-ready tape. In order to segregate these costs, we called the firm that had produced the microfilm from the tape that WLN had provided of our holdings. The actual microfilm cost: $334. Our bill from WLN: $3,522.47.

The next question was obvious—could the vendor, rather than WLN, provide the same service from a tape that our library would provide. The answer was along the line of, "Do I care who sends the tape as long as your check clears?" Since this $3,500 charge for a COM update was based on 75,000 of our estimated 100,000 titles, we suddenly realized that an integrated system that was capable of sorting the database could save us between $4,000 and $5,000 for each COM cumulation! The *LJ* buying guide issue turned up several more possibilities for inexpensive MARC records, including MARCIVE in San Antonio. They could provide bits and bytes at $.11 each. They agreed to attempt to proceed via a dial-up arrangement rather than sending magnetic tapes through the mail.

Meanwhile, our best efforts had managed to wring but $75,000 out of the City for the circulation system. However, we reasoned that: (1) with automated circulation we would effect some staff savings and generate some extra cash, (2) vendor prices on a competitive bid would be substantially less than what we were hearing from their marketing people, and (3) the savings from WLN could be applied toward the new system's costs.

## *THE RFP*

So with high hopes and a low budget we began to think about preparation of a Request For Proposals (RFP), and the need for a consultant. Consultants in the area of library automation typically provide four services: (1) instant technical expertise, (2) handholding, (3) a scapegoat, if things go wrong, and (4) a fund of knowledge/

scuttlebutt concerning the less technical side of automation. Our low budget meant that someone from the library would have to provide the above services. Since there was no one on the library staff who knew anything about automation, it became obvious that the Library Director would have to acquire the expertise, since the rest of the staff had all they could do to keep normal library functions operating.

In our search for other available free expertise, we turned first to the City's data-processing department. To their credit, the initial reaction wasn't "Don't worry, we can write a program in three to four weeks that will run on the City computer." They took the time to learn that a library system would be difficult to program, degrade response time, and use up much of the available disk storage space on their new WANG VS system. In the end, they replied that, while it might be possible to share some of their peripheral equipment if we found a library system written for the WANG, they weren't enthusiastic about the idea.

We next turned to the local newspaper's DP department for advice. Like City Hall, the newspaper was close enough to the library so that a timesharing arrangement on their computer might be possible. Initially we were encouraged. Their staff was quick to understand our situation. They had DEC hardware, which was used by several vendors and, at that time, excess capacity on their three PDP-1170 processors. They also had more than an ample amount of disk storage and they were accustomed to the kind of data retrieval that occurs in a library. They hinted that the newspaper management might be interested in translating their excess capacity into some revenue through a timesharing arrangement so we decided to include a timeshare option in our RFP.

The next step was to write the Request For Proposals. Since ours was a low-budget operation, we asked colleagues from larger libraries who had recently been through this process to send a copy of their RFPs. We soon had a truly intimidating stack of documents. On closer examination, they seemed to be 95 percent boilerplate, and used the same legalese/computerese. Then came another revelation. Three books recommended by a nearby librarian turned out to be the source of most of the boiler plate. So after a major cut and paste operation, we produced an imposing document and sent it over to City Hall.

The RFP reflected the assumption that we had two alternatives: (1) buy a simple circulation only system, and retain our membership in WLN, or (2) buy an integrated system and drop WLN. If the latter were to happen, the new system would have to:

1. Be able to connect with MARCIVE via a dial-up telephone line to retrieve and process those cheap MARC records.
2. Sort the database and produce a print-ready tape for the production of 16mm COM film for our readers.
3. Provide prompted catalog entry screens, hopefully with an authority control feature.
4. Include a circulation subsystem.
5. Include an acquisition subsystem with fund accounting.

In response to our RFP, at the appointed hour, the designated person publicly opened the boxes and we anxiously scanned the executive summaries for the bottom line. To our chagrin, the bottom lines were all qualified by assumptions of one sort or another. After a week of reading and calculating, we finally arrived at the point where the entire process was reduced to one sheet of paper, with a few qualifications of our own such as: System A did not include a tape drive, System B included a tape drive because it was essential to files backup, and System C included a tape drive as an option. In this example, since we had not specified a tape drive as a requirement, the cost was added to the total acquisition and maintenance cost of System B only.

The cost analysis included the following elements. First, we established the cost of continued membership in WLN, and developed a set of assumptions as to additional staff that would be added if circulation increased by X percent. Second, each vendor's purchase cost and five year operational cost was calculated. From this we subtracted anticipated staff savings. Then, if the system did not provide the features necessary to allow us to drop WLN, the latter costs were added for a five year period. Unfortunately, long before we finalized the analysis, it became apparent that none of the bids were really satisfactory for a cost that we could afford and we were forced to reject all of them. We notified bidders accordingly.

A number of lessons that should have been perfectly obvious to us bear mentioning. The Everett Public was small potatoes as automated system sales are concerned. We drew this conclusion from the fact that responses to our RFP appear to have been pumped out of word processors irrespective of differences in the way we wanted certain functions handled. The second lesson was that we expected lower prices on a competitive bid than what we had heard from their sales people. Not so; if anything bid prices were higher.

## DILEMMA RESOLVED

At the time that spirits were lowest, a marvelous thing happened. A local businessman appeared at the library, and donated $75,000. He made but two conditions on his gift: That he remain anonymous and that savings from the system be allocated for books. We made some minor changes to the RFP, pushed it through the City Hall Xerox machine a second time, and waited for the response—this time with the clear confidence that we had the money in the bank and could afford an integrated system if one surfaced. When the bids were opened and analyzed, Easy Data Systems, now Sidney Development Corporation, was chosen as both the most responsive and the one providing least cost over five years.

Several months later the Library Board voted to cancel the contract with WLN after reviewing cost data. Updated to reflect actual 1985 figures, those costs would now look like this:

*ANNUAL COSTS SUMMARY*:

Washington Library Network (1985 estimates)
| | |
|---|---:|
| Cataloging | $23,906.00 |
| Acquisition | 4,650.00 |
| Interlibrary Loan (costs incl. above) | 0.00 |
| TOTAL | $28,556.00 |

Easy Data Systems (1985 actual)
| | |
|---|---:|
| Cataloging | $1,192.41 |
| Acquisition | 50.00 |
| Interlibrary Loan | 600.00 |
| TOTAL | $1,842.41 |

In this comparison, hardware and software for our local system are not included due to the fact that we would incur these costs for circulation regardless of the WLN decision. The question before the library was whether we should continue WLN membership at an additional cost of $28,000+ per year, or drop WLN and rely on the Easy Data software and MARCIVE. The decision was whether the added services, resource sharing/ILL and shared cataloging, were worth the added costs.

At this point we learned the value of the time we had spent in the preparation of our long-range plan. In 1981 the library followed its own version of the PLA Planning Process, and had developed a five year plan and a mission statement:

> The mission of the Everett Public Library is to make readily available the most wanted library materials to all those who use the library, to serve as an access point for any needed information, and to provide these services at an affordable cost.

This Baltimore County derived mission statement, and the sometimes practical sometimes philosophical discussion that preceded it have given the staff and trustees a sense of focus that has been extremely helpful in addressing both old and new policy questions. So it was from this framework that we examined the decision regarding WLN.

ILL still operates, philosophically, in the pre-computer days when the logistical difficulties involved in locating a book for a patron inhibited its use. Although the Pacific Northwest had one of the few workable union catalog finding systems in the country, the paperwork and the time delays kept the system in check. Now virtually every library in the state can afford a fiche reader and the $300 cost of WLN's holdings in fiche. Libraries serving a population of 5,000 or less pay only $150. Some questions need answers:

1. What are the long-range consequences of spending funds for access to books which were bought with the tax dollars of other communities rather than spending this money for more books?
2. What happens when the larger libraries simply say, "Enough! If you want to use our books, the cost is $_____"?
3. When #2 happens will budgets be configured such that selection librarians choose between paying $7.00 to use a book, or paying $14.00 for the book itself?
4. What is wrong with telling our patrons that we need more money to buy books?

Everyone in the profession realizes that resources sharing is an expensive philosophy. Two logical questions remain: (1) Do we need it? and (2) Who should pay? The clear answer is certainly not the lender!

The second network service that Everett would lose if we dropped WLN was shared cataloging. As in other networks, members contribute cataloging to the database, which is then available to all other members. We estimated that something between five to eight percent of cataloging for new titles was member contributed. Based on our average new title acquisition rate of 4,000 per year, this would mean the loss of cataloging for 200 to 320 titles. This did not seem to be a serious matter.

So we cancelled our contract with WLN. While there were side issues, the real reason was cost. Given the present rate structures of WLN and OCLC, only larger libraries can justify the expenditure for such an online service. Unfortunately there doesn't seem to be any interest in developing a different/cheaper approach to network participation. A recent study by Peat, Marwick & Mitchell (1984) of WLN's future markets and services didn't even mention the notion of a different service and rate structure for smaller libraries. We regard cataloging as another overhead cost, just like the phone bill and the heat bill. If we found a cheaper way to heat the building, we would change tomorrow. Why should network costs be viewed any differently?

## *DECISION REVIEWED*

Now, two and one-half years later it is possible to reflect on our odyssey and offer some thoughts on libraries, networks, and automation. There has to be a renewed focus for public libraries on their mission to their respective publics. In Everett's case, this is translated into a concentration of effort to determine what our readers want/need, and then to allocate our resources to meet those needs. As a result, 20.6 percent of the 1985 operating budget was spent on books.

Second, when involved in a network, one catalogs to network standards. Network standards (MARC/LSCH) presume that cataloging that is adequate for the largest research library is also appropriate for a small public library. Not so! While it has taken time to unlearn some things and clear the head of network standards, we are now beginning to understand that cataloging must be useful for the public we serve.

Third, networks have made cataloging an even more arcane science than the 3 × 5 era of our profession, and in many cases the reference/public service staff are even further from their basic tool for serving the public than before. However, based on our experience with a local integrated system, the opposite is taking place. Our staff now understands more about cataloging than ever before.

Fourth, while we spent a great deal of time searching for a source of cheap MARC records, we do not store full MARC records in the system. MARC is, as Henriette Avram (1984) stated in a letter to *LJ*, a communications format. Put another way, it is a convention that facilitates the exchange of bibliographic records in much the same way that eggs are bought and sold by the dozen. Unfortunately, some librarians are under the mistaken impression that they need to store and use these full MARC records for their local applications. This is particularly unfortunate among the small and medium libraries; it is analogous to the conclusion that since eggs are bought by the dozen, they should be used by the dozen. Based on the disk storage requirements of some automated systems, some librarians have concluded that they not only need to cook a dozen eggs for their two egg omelet appetite, but they are throwing in the carton for good measure.

Fifth, the time we saved in the automated system selection process caught up with us at the time of implementation. At this point, the staff had to learn the basics of electronic data processing. Some needed to know more, some wanted to know more, but everyone had to have a basic understanding of how automation works. Inadequate documentation and poorly conceived training from our vendor lengthened the process as well.

Networks provide three primary services—access to LC MARC records, shared cataloging, and interlibrary loan. The Everett Public Library felt that these services were priced beyond our means and acted accordingly. Now that vendors besides MARCIVE are providing cheap MARC records in other formats, especially in compact disks, perhaps other libraries will follow our suit. We certainly hope so, because very few large bureaucratic institutions, like networks, change of their own accord. They change only with the threat of economic extinction. Linkages among libraries are important, but the cost must be affordable, and in proportion to the benefits.

## REFERENCES

Avram, Henrietta. "MARC or the Marketplace," *Library Journal* 109 (July 1984), p. 1268.
Franklin, Ralph and Claire I. MacDonald. "The Washington Library Network," *Special Libraries* 67 (February 1976), pp. 84-90.
Peat, Marwick, Mitchell. *The Washington Library Network: Long-Range Service Plan and Organizational Alternatives, February, 1984*. San Francisco: Peat, Marwick, Mitchell, March 30, 1984.

# Linking CLSI and UTLAS to Meet Local Needs

## Polly Coe

When I graduated from library school in 1969, automation was an expensive luxury that few but the best funded libraries could even consider. In 1985, the world of library automation is substantially different from what it was then. There are library systems available on minicomputers and microcomputers that are affordable for all size libraries.

When I was appointed Director at Gainsville three years ago, the library had no database and no automation, not even a word processor. Instead it had a circulation system that was designed to handle less than half of its current load and that, in spite of the unceasing efforts of a most diligent staff, repeatedly lost books, reserves, even patrons. It had long since stopped being any sort of inventory control and required exponential increases in staff to type overdues and file in no less than 49 manual files. The circulation function was in a crisis. Thanks to a history of meager book budgets the acquisitions/cataloging functions were not in the same sort of situation, although here too there were problems including a cumbersome divided catalog that befuddled the public and would have required massive staff time to convert to dictionary format; a card catalog that was growing beyond the space available; and a history of rather typical quick and dirty public library cataloging that often did not satisfy local needs.

Luckily, by 1982, the automation of library functions was no longer for the wealthy among us, since Gainsville needed help. As with most medium size libraries, our two largest budget items are personnel at $1,092,960, or 70 percent of the total operating budget in 1984-85, and books and materials at $275,000 or 18 percent of the budget. Automated library systems could help resolve our problems by offering one mechanism to: (1) increase access to holdings

---

Polly Coe, Director, Alachua County Public Library, Gainsville, FL 32601.

© 1986 by The Haworth Press, Inc. All rights reserved.

without increasing the cataloging/acquisitions staff; and (2) increase circulation transactions without increasing staff to type overdues, search for reserves, and file in growing manual files.

## DECIDING THE PRIORITIES

Before writing system specifications or preparing a Request for Proposal (RFP), we decided to educate ourselves. Although all things may be possible with the computer, we assumed that we might only be able to afford the high priority items. So we needed to know what was available and at what cost before we could prioritize our library's needs for potential vendors. We scoured the literature, of course; but, frankly, the literature tends to be a bit rosy. Human nature is such that it does not wish to reveal errors of judgment in a public forum. We looked at various systems available—at conferences and in-house so that all interested staff could see them. But, most importantly, we visited libraries that had already automated, regardless of what system or systems they were using. We took a variety of staff so that the cataloger could talk to their catalogers, the reference librarian to their reference staff, etc.

The visits clarified our priorities and what aspects of automation would most benefit our library before we sat down with a systems analyst from the City to design the specifications. Although we had learned that there was not really any 100 percent integrated system, we knew we wanted a system that was as integrated as possible. For example, one library we visited had three separate data entry points for every new title—an online ordering system to place and track orders; a bibliographic utility to pick up full MARC data, produce COM catalogs, and to network ILLs; and a completely separate circulation system.

Most libraries we visited raved about their networks, but few could document for us cost savings that were transferable to our situation. What saves money for the University of Florida libraries would not necessarily save our public library money. Consider resource sharing and interlibrary loans which amounted to 820 in 1984 in Gainsville as compared to a 829,383 circulation for the same year. Although we might dream professionally of a world in which every library, no matter how small, makes available every resource in the country to its users, our reality is that what our user most wants is more books, more copies of heavy demand titles, more newspapers and periodicals, i.e., more of what we are already providing. It was clear to us that our priority must be to increase existing resources. For this medium size public library the costs of networking for the purpose of resource sharing became clearly a low priority at least for the immediate future.

In one area, networking offered a clear benefit to our library in cost savings. Not having a database we were obviously going to have to perform a retrospective conversion. During our research, one of the vendors gave us an estimate of the workforce required. Our experience has since confirmed that adding local holdings data to an already existent MARC record takes three minutes of paraprofessional staff time per title, while doing original cataloging in MARC format takes 30 minutes of professional staff time per title. It does not take a mathematician to understand that efficiency. We concluded that a network, or bibliographic utility, was an efficient option for the RECON project.

## COSTING THE PROJECT

We decided to cost the entire project once and subsequently request funding for it, including the database conversion and an integrated library automation system. We sampled our shelf list and asked all networks to give us hit rate percentages for their database. We used this information to estimate the number of temporary staff needed and their job levels for the conversion project, and to estimate a reasonable schedule for the project. Surprisingly, not all networks would bid. Some would supply guesstimates over the phone, but would not commit themselves in writing. Since we were hoping to get all of the necessary money needed to fund the effort at one time, we were uncomfortable with guesstimates that could well lead to the type of cost overruns that are more typically associated with the Pentagon than public libraries. Indeed, some network staff implied that we were expecting too much in asking them to commit to a hit rate or a specific budget.

## GOING OUT FOR BIDS

Our RFP was split into two sections that vendors could bid on separately or together: (1) retrospective conversion for full MARC and current MARC cataloging on a shared database to both maintain the card catalog through the project and to put new acquisitions into the database; and (2) a turnkey integrated library system for circulation control, Public Access Catalog, acquisitions and cataloging. We thought that we were clear in the RFP that we wanted only one conversion project, but we received bids that would have required two conversions. Because of inaccuracies in our shelf list, we knew that we would have to do our conversion from the books. Therefore, we wanted to handle the books only once, and enter the holdings into the database at the same time we pulled the MARC record. What seemed obvious to us was apparently somewhat revolutionary to the bidders. That was not surprising, since Don Sager (1981) pointed out when he was President of the American Library Association's Public Library Division (ALA-PLA) that public libraries had taken little part in the initiation of networks and were now feeling the results. We selected a joint bid from a network, UTLAS, and a turnkey vendor, CLSI, who were creative and worked out what we needed, recognizing that there are a lot of libraries in the country in our situation, i.e., with no database on which to build an automated system. They bridged that often unintegrated gap between MARC data from a network to in-house database and got our contract. It is not a perfect interface. The MARC tapes are mailed to us, because the online interconnection is still under development. However, in analyzing costs, the brief delay to receive tapes was a fair trade-off to be able to avoid either two conversions or two data entry steps.

The reason we were so adamant about putting into operation the most integrated system possible was to save money in direct staff time. There is no perfect library automation system. Each library must analyze what its priorities are and the aim of automation for it. In our case, the crisis in circulation control had to be our first priority. Therefore, we wanted a fully tested and proved circulation system with reserves, overdues and fines. We were also planning for growth—increased book budget, increased branches, etc. Future savings were bound up with the number of support staff needed in circulation and cataloging. The Public Access Catalog seemed to us originally a somewhat luxurious service enhancement to which we might some day upgrade, but if we reach our goals of additional branches and a greatly increased book budget, the online catalog could quickly become the least expensive option to provide the public with access to the collection. Therefore, the Public Access Catalog became a higher priority in our RFP.

Networking has good and bad aspects. For example, the average medium size public library doesn't need the MARC record to open access to its collection for users. We insisted on MARC records, because we do offer our citizens interlibrary loans for materials we do not own. We send a staff member twice a week to the University of Florida Libraries, and we mail ILL forms to the State Library. When it becomes cost efficient, we will have the option of online access to other libraries. In other words, we did not want to limit future network options, even though the options are not available to us now.

## SHARED CATALOGING VIA A NETWORK

The final aspect of networking is the use of UTLAS for shared cataloging of current acquisitions. For the duration of our RECON project, we decided to maintain the card catalog and continue adding cards for new acquisitions. The options were to: (1) have staff continue producing card sets in-house while also inputting new acquisitions into the data base; or (2) have the network produce the cards to free staff time. Gainsville selected the latter. The cost of current cataloging is high, there are connect time charges, charges for added entries, for original cataloging and charges for communications.

Gainsville is half way through the year and one-half conversion project; we are uneasily watching the cost of current cataloging via UTLAS climb. While our decision to use a network for current cataloging through the conversion project remains a good choice, we are considering dropping network cataloging after the RECON is complete. About 75 to 80 percent of our library's current acquisitions have Library of Congress CIP. The question we must answer is, "Would it be cheaper for us to simply do our own MARC cataloging than to purchase shared cataloging from a network?" Frankly, we do not know yet, but we will be comparing the costs for the next year. Right now it seems quite possible that the answer will be yes and that we will drop the network at least for a couple of years until we are ready to increase acquisitions a good deal for new facilities. Increased purchasing might make network shared cataloging more cost efficient than it is at our current level of purchasing.

Automation has greatly increased the complexity of administrative decision making. Each library functions in a specific environment that is unique to it. Two libraries of similar type, size, and community may choose very different paths for quite valid reasons.

Costing current cataloging through a network from Gainsville, Florida will produce very different telecommunications costs than those of a library in closer proximity to network headquarters. Networking is not a panacea or universal cure-all. It is only useful in so far as it saves a specific library money or adds needed resources for a library's users at a cost the library can justify.

## REFERENCE

Sager, Donald J. "Library Automation for the Urban Public Library: Problems and Solutions." In: Alex Ladenson, Editor. *Current Trends in Library Automation*. Chicago: Urban Libraries Council, 1981, pp. 1-24.

# Present and Future Network Base for New Mexico's Public Libraries

Ed Sayre

New Mexico librarians adopted their first long-range plan for statewide library services in 1971; they called it Coordinated Library Systems (CLS). Like most state library long-range plans, CLS emphasized resource sharing and interlibrary cooperation.

New Mexico has some distinct geographic and demographic features, and it has some unique social problems. It is a large state, 121,666 square miles. In 1971, it had an unevenly distributed population of 1,016,000 with an average of 8.35 persons per square mile. The average income for a New Mexico family ranked 44th among the 50 states; education, health, and social services were below national standards; and the state was—and is—made up of three cultures, Indian, Hispanic, and Anglo, with consequent inequities in opportunity.

Library resources throughout the state were slim. In its comparatively brief history as a state, appropriations for library services, both state and local, had been meager. There were no bastions of library strength developed over the years. Even the University of New Mexico and the Albuquerque Public Library were, by comparative standards, weak. Other university and public libraries could provide only marginal services and resources.

The librarians, trustees, and other interested citizens who created CLS realized the difficulties of delivering library services in the New Mexico environment. At the same time, they realized the importance of library and information services for New Mexico's people. Those working on CLS thought that improved library and information services could help alleviate, if not solve, the state's social, economic, and educational problems. An underlying assumption of CLS was one of the fudamental justifications for interlibrary cooperation and resource sharing: All residents of New Mexico should

Ed Sayre, director, Los Alamos County Library, Los Alamos, NM 87544.

© 1986 by The Haworth Press, Inc. All rights reserved.

have reasonable access to all publicly procured library materials regardless of the location of the resident or the location of the materials.

## RESOURCE SHARING IN NEW MEXICO

The necessary ingredients for interlibrary cooperation and resource sharing are: A means of knowing the location of desired materials, a communication system between locations, and a delivery service between locations (Becker, 1971; Kent and Galvin, 1977 and 1979). In implementing CLS, the New Mexico State Library, in consultation with librarians throughout the state, decided to attack the second ingredient first by using teletype communications between four university libraries and the State Library. In 1974, using LSCA Title I funds, it expanded that network to include 12 of the larger public libraries in the state; there were only 39 established at the time. The protocol for interlibrary requests was essentially a polling routine. Without knowing the location of the materials sought, the requesting librarians sent initial requests to a scheduled library in the protocol sequence; that library filled what it could and relayed the remainder of the request to a second, third, fourth, fifth library, and so on. This system was, of course, inefficient and only partially effective, but, given the technology of the times and the limited funds available, it was a reasonable approach to perceived needs. The librarians' reactions to the system were generally enthusiastic. It was a new experience for people who, for whatever reasons, might have felt isolated; they developed a feeling of involvement. Some public library directors were so enthusiastic they put their teletype machines in the middle of the library so the public could see how they were connected to the rest of the world. The teletype service enhanced staff members' sense of professional involvement.

But, after just a few years, the enthusiam began to wear thin. The time required to support the system, the limited successes, the realization that alternative systems were available—mainly online services—prompted participating librarians to question the continued validity of the teletype network. One fact that piqued the interest in online services was the availability of OCLC in the university libraries, where they had been procured through a state appropriation. Public librarians began to consider the possibilities for OCLC in their network, and were anxious to obtain better access to the universities' holdings.

In 1980, the New Mexico State Librarian and the Legislative Committee of the New Mexico Library Association began working on proposals for installation of OCLC in selected public libraries throughout the state. The working group gave almost no consideration to other networking alternatives, because all six of the state university libraries, holding publicly procured materials, had already installed OCLC and had put many of their records in the utility's database. The Committee selected 14 of the now 41 public libraries for installation. After considerable preparation and political hustling, the group won an appropriation of $165,000 for 14 terminals. AMIGOS, as the regional OCLC representative, made the installation, provided the training, and contracted for services. With this event, there were 20 publicly supported university and public libraries in the state with OCLC. There are now 35 OCLC participants in the state, including federal, state, municipal, and privately owned libraries.

Cataloging services became available to the public libraries in the fall of 1980. The interlibrary loan network was operational in December of 1980. A very informal protocol for interlibrary loan was negotiated to conform to AMIGOS' rules and to emphasize use of in-state resources. The State Library, in addition to paying for initial purchase and installation costs, now pays the AMIGOS' membership fees and the telecommunications costs for those 14 public libraries. The State Library, therefore, allocates about $70,000 a year from its operating budget to support public library networking. The individual libraries pay only for the transaction costs.

## *THE LOS ALAMOS CONNECTION*

Los Alamos County occupies the site of the Manhattan Project which developed and built the atomic bombs that were dropped on Hiroshima and Nagasaki. After World War II, the Manhattan Project Laboratory was retained by the federal government and converted to one of the major national laboratories of the United States. In 1949, Los Alamos became a home rule city-county of the state of New Mexico. The public library—called the Mesa Public Library—which had previously operated under contract for federal employees, became a part of Los Alamos County government.

Los Alamos County is a unique governmental entity, because it is almost wholly dependent on the national laboratory as an economic base; it is a one industry town. The laboratory requires a highly educated staff, and, accordingly, pays generously to attract scientists and support personnel to this remote area for employment. The Los Alamos population of 19,000 is, therefore, both well educated and affluent. They put a high value on public library services and have supported the public library well since it became a part of local government. At this writing, the public library has a budget of about $735,000, roughly $39.00 per capita, from the general tax revenues of the County. Because of this kind of support, the Los Alamos County Library has accumulated a respectable collection of over 104,000 volumes. There are no chronological gaps in the collection because of any particular years of economic decline.

Because of its collection, Los Alamos has always been a heavy lender in New Mexico's interlibrary loan network. Also because of its demanding clientele, Los Alamos has been a heavy borrower from state and national interlibrary loan networks. For many years during the decade of the 70s and the early 80s, Los Alamos loaned and borrowed more items than any other public library in the state, including Albuquerque. The library staff was naturally enthusiastic about OCLC for, among other reasons, expectations of an improved hit rate for interlibrary loan. With its massive database, OCLC fulfilled those expectations. Where we once had a hit rate of about 65 percent with the teletype system, OCLC gave us almost 100 percent. And, of course, it had additional advantages of reducing paperwork, reducing time for confirmation of loans, and reducing delivery time for receipt of materials.

The Los Alamos County Library staff made full use of the cataloging and interlibrary loan networks as soon as they were available in the fall of 1980. We went into an aggressive training program to qualify as many staff members as practical in OCLC applications. OCLC gave us all a lift. It provided new experiences and gave us hopes of increased effectiveness and efficiency. Again, one of the most distinct advantages was the enhanced sense of professional involvement that staff members felt. We began to realize, more and more, that we were not a single library isolated in the mountains of northern New Mexico, but that we were an integral part of the world of library and information services. There is no way to put a dollar value on this kind of spin-off, but it means a great deal at all levels of the staff hierarchy.

## OCLC AND RECON

The Los Alamos County Library enjoys high circulation of materials, about 275,000 a year, or about 14.5 per capita; we have about 25 percent of our collection in circulation at any one time. For several years, the staff had been discussing the possibilities of developing an online circulation and inventory control system. That was the most important component of our long-range plans for computer applications in the library. The first major task for the system, of course, would be conversion of the card catalog to machine readable form.

After considerable investigation, we finally decided to use OCLC for the retrospective conversion process. There were several important considerations in this decision: We would not have to go out to bid for a contract and go through the cost of contract monitoring and administration; we could use our own staff which was demonstrably reliable and enthusiastic; we would have on-site supervision; and, perhaps most important, we could be flexible with OCLC, slowing down when necessary and accelerating when desirable. We enlisted the entire library staff—including the director—to work on the retrospective conversion and scheduled them for all available/non-prime time hours, Monday through Saturday. We worked on that schedule from August 1981 to July 1983, almost two years. Predictably, we had about a 98 percent hit rate, so there were comparatively few snags and rather few original entries for the OCLC database.

The decision to enlist the full staff for work on a project that was the exclusive responsibility of the Technical Services Divisions turned out to be an extremely fortunate move. Staff members began to learn more about cataloging and, hence, developed a greater appreciation of the role of technical services personnel. This use of the network served to bring the staff together, to strengthen our sense of mutual support, to generally improve morale, and, again, to enhance our sense of professionalism. We had no trouble getting volunteers, even in the off hours, and everyone was able to share in the pride of participating in an important job. Personnel augmented costs for the retrospective conversion came to about $12,000 that included the planning, training, supervision, and actual loading. Transaction costs were about $14,000. We bought the archival tapes for less than $1,000. The OCLC retrospective conversion expense was certainly money well spent. We obtained the records necessary for the bar code collation for the circulation system; we had records available for an eventual online catalog; we had made our entire catalog available for OCLC's interlibrary loan network; and we gave the staff an excellent education in library and computer technology. That $27,000 investment of public funds had served the taxpayers well.

In July 1983, the county administration decided we would develop a local, tailor-made circulation and inventory control system rather than go to a commercial vendor. Both the library staff and the library board opposed this decision, but the administration's choice prevailed. We did our best in working with the County Management Information Services Department, and after a year and a half, the system was installed and operational by January, 1985. All things considered, it is a good system with some custom features that might not have been available from a commercial source.

## *EFFECTIVENESS AND EFFICIENCY*

In deciding to adopt any process for a library system, the director must think in terms of effectiveness and efficiency. For New Mexico, and certainly for the Los Alamos County Library, both the OCLC cataloging and interlibrary loan networks have been highly effective. They have veritably put us in a new world of technical support for the patrons and the staff.

It is not so easy to make claims for the efficiency of OCLC in New Mexico. Efficiency, in this context, must entail consideration of a cost-benefit ratio. Are the benefits of OCLC greater in value than the costs? We all understand the difficulties of making that determination, but certain facts are apparent. The most important fact is that a favorable cost-benefit ratio depends, in large part, on economies of scale, i.e., the greater the number of transactions through the system, the lower the ultimate cost for each transaction. We have done a cost analysis of interlibrary loan transactions using OCLC in Los Alamos. That analysis has included a formulated distribution of such costs as OCLC membership, telecommunications, staff time, materials, and overhead. The current cost to us for receiving a book on interlibrary loan from another library—where our patron is the beneficiary—is about $11.14. As stated earlier, we borrow about 1,000 items a year. If we want to reduce costs for this service, we must either cut the costs for the service components, e.g., salaries, materials, or we must increase the number of transactions, with a proportionately lower increase in the distributed costs. Neither alternative seems readily available. The question arises: Is an interlibrary loan delivery worth $11.14 to the patron, and, indirectly, to the library? We think it is. All users of interlibrary loans have expressed satisfaction with the service. The power of the OCLC utility, considered in conjunction with other service modes, has increased both the effectiveness and the efficiency of the interlibrary loan service in Los Alamos.

But there are other considerations which have not gone into our cost analysis. The most notable is that we have not calculated the value of Los Alamos lending 1,000 items to other libraries, most of them in New Mexico. Considering the ubiquity of taxation in this country, it seems perfectly appropriate that we should share our resources. We think it is just good, practical, public relations; we take a certain amount of pride in our ability to help others. There is no way of quantifying that benefit. At the very least, we feel we are doing our share to compensate for the State Library's contribution to our OCLC services.

Analyzing cataloging costs, using OCLC, is as problematical as analyzing interlibrary loan costs. Our analysis tells us we can currently process a book for about $10.34. That is acceptable. We doubt we could bring that cost down and still maintain a quality product by abandoning OCLC. With a new branch library, we processed over 10,000 items last fiscal year. We expect to maintain that schedule in the foreseeable future. It is hard to imagine how we could operate the Technical Services Division effectively and efficiently without OCLC, or something comparable, even if we had to pay for the telecommunications and membership fees now paid for by the State Library.

## *CONTRIBUTIONS AND THE FUTURE*

And that brings up the final point. None of the other libraries in New Mexico, for whatever reasons, has loaded its catalog in a retrospective conversion process into the OCLC database. The public libraries, because of low budgets, have not made substantial contributions of new acquisitions. Albuquerque Public Library, with the largest acquisitions budget among public libraries in the state, spends much of its appropriation on duplicate titles because of the number of its branches. After four and one half years, there are about 300,000 public library records, not unique, in the OCLC database from New Mexico's public libraries. The duplication rate is probably high regardless of the individuality of those involved in collection development. Consequently, only 27 percent of the items borrowed by public libraries in New Mexico comes from other public libraries in New Mexico through the OCLC network.

One of the goals for investment in OCLC for public libraries was to increase interlibrary loan traffic among them. Whether the goal has practical or just philosophical relevance is moot. So the cost-benefit ratio of the State Library investment has to be called into question. Are there enough interlibrary loan or cataloging transactions to justify the expenditure of $70,000 a year for support of OCLC in New Mexico? Individual public libraries may justify their own expenses for OCLC, but, as an intrastate network it is doubtful the benefits have exceeded the costs. It is difficult to ascertain at what transaction volume the costs would be justified; further, it is dubious that most public libraries could attain that transaction volume. With increases in telecommunications' costs imminent, the prospects for expense justification seem even less likely.

For all that, the interlude with OCLC has been advantageous. It has been a good learning experience and we have benefited in many unquantifiable ways. But the trend of dependency on national utilities seems to be waning. Despite the unquestionable universality of the library enterprise and the impressive capabilities of national bibliographic utilities, most librarians seem to feel more comfortable working in regional systems and networks. More and more library agencies are looking to new alignments for networking possibilities. Interested librarians in New Mexico are searching for alternatives to OCLC or for alternatives within OCLC itself. One of the more attractives that has emerged since we made the original investment in OCLC is laser disk catalog bases conjoined with electronic mail systems, which may provide some solutions. It yet remains to work out a system design that will accommodate the needs of all New Mexico's public libraries.

## REFERENCES

Becker, Joseph, Editor. *Conference on Interlibrary Communication and Information Networks, 1970, Proceedings.* Chicago: American Library Association, 1971.

Kent, Allen and Thomas J. Galvin, Editors. *Library Resource Sharing.* New York: Marcel Dekker, 1977.

──────. *The Structure and Governance of Library Networks.* New York: Marcel Dekker, 1979.

# Networking at the Principal Public Library in Rhode Island: A Decade of Change

Annalee M. Bundy

The Providence Public Library (PPL) serves a population of almost 1,000,000 people in its role as the Principal Public Library of Rhode Island. In addition to its Central Library, there are seven branches and one affiliate library.

The role of Principal Public Library makes Providence responsible for interlibrary loan throughout the state, as a result the Library provides the delivery system and acts as a switching station for all requests from other public, academic, school and special libraries. Most of the requests were originally sent either by teletype or by written communication. The old teletype was replaced recently by an electronic mail system. Before the requests reach Providence, however, they have been searched at two local levels, that is, within the originating library and then within that institution's region. Many are subject requests which are more complicated to fill than a specific title request. Forms are used that allow the requester to provide as much information as necessary to locate the type of material that is needed. There is also space to note what has been searched to date.

## ONLINE CIRCULATION, ACQUISITIONS AND PUBLIC ACCESS CATALOG

The PPL, computerized with a circulation system that has been in operation since 1973 and a book acquisition system that had its beginnings in 1972, was an early entry into the automation arena. The two subsystems both from CLSI, were tied together in 1982, so that

---

Annalee M. Bundy, Director, Providence Public Library, Providence, RI 02903.

the library is online for both acquisitions and circulation. The library also has a CLSI Public Access Catalog which is linked to the other two automated modules. This is scheduled to be expanded further in 1986.

In initially looking at bibliographic utilities nearly a decade ago the PPL was most concerned with ongoing costs as well as with services provided. Services that were desired were cataloging and interlibrary loan information. However, the need was greatest for up-to-date cataloging with card production. Interlibrary loan was of secondary importance. It was not easy to suit the needs of the PPL. Since public libraries had only limited involvement in networking at its inception, available services were often not appropriate. Sager (1981) has pointed out the irony of this situation, since the major support needed for network survival frequently came from LSCA funding which had as its function improvement of public library services.

Providence was doing customized cataloging for almost every item, because the library used a Dewey Decimal Classification but transposed the 300's and 800's. This required that a high proportion of the numbers be original; standard LC card classification numbers would not work. Subject heading were a mixture of local and standard LC subject headings.

Cards were printed in-house and reproduced as needed. That is, often all branches did not order a particular title at the same time, which meant that some sets of cards were produced on demand. To print cards a master was made and then overlays were put on the main card for additional subject headings. A master would print up to two hundred copies of a card, but rarely if ever were two hundred copies needed. Masters were only kept for a short time, meaning that if a branch ordered an added title a few months after other branches or the Central Library, a new master had to be made even for three cards. This was an expensive means of card production. It was decided that the library would use a photocopy machine instead of printing. Still the high cost and appearance left much to be desired; another means was sought. During this time, the book budget doubled and a backlog of uncataloged books was the result. Staff size did not grow in proportion to the book budget so an easier, more efficient means was sought to provide cataloging information and cards. Three full-time professsionals and one part-time professional worked in the cataloging department. They were assisted by several clerks who handled typing, filing, and book and card processing.

Providence looked into the most accessible bibliographic utility available at the time; it was OCLC using NELINET. Cost of being a member plus the cards was in the vicinity of $22,000 for the first year and about $18,000 to $20,000 per year after start-up. The cataloging was neater and there was an added benefit for interlibrary loan purposes with the academic libraries and special libraries that were OCLC members. No Rhode Island public libraries or school libraries were members of OCLC, however. Because of PPL's complex system, classifications were still done locally. The basic need remained cataloging at the most affordable price with cards readily available.

## MINI-MARC FOR CATALOGING AND CARD PRODUCTION

The alternative that presented itself in 1980 was to purchase outright a MINI-MARC System for cataloging and card production. The cost was about $55,000 initially with an annual subscription rate and maintenance fee of $12,000. This, of course, did not provide complete MARC records in every case, nor did it provide interlibrary loan possibilities. What it did allow was a direct tie in with the library's acquisitions system and the circulation control system. It also permitted branches to get cards whenever they ordered a book simply by calling up the author and title on the index of the MINI-MARC and then loading the proper diskette into the processor to produce a card set exactly like all the others in the system. While this may not appear to others as the ideal, it did meet the need in Providence.

In deciding whether to use a bibliographic utility, it was felt that cataloging requirements could be met using MINI-MARC which cost far less over a five year period. The costs for MINI-MARC could also be controlled. If, through some unforeseen situation, the budget was drastically cut, withdrawing the subscription and service contract from MINI-MARC would not create serious problems for the library, which would have been the case with a bibliographic utility.

The public is generally not concerned with catalogs or cataloging formats. Only about four or five percent of Providence patrons ever look in the catalog even though Providence is a research library. So, belonging to a bibliographic utility is of little or no concern to the average user. The public catalog may change use patterns, however.

Younger constituents, particularly, like the touch screen and keyboard. Possibly the novelty is what interests them more than the information. Once the pattern of using an online catalog is established, hopefully it will continue as a lifelong habit.

## RECON FOR GREATER PUBLIC ACCESS

It is now almost five years since PPL purchased MINI-MARC and the library is embarking on a new venture. With a grant from a private foundation the library is retrospectively converting all of its records and those of the other libraries on its circulation system, which contains over 375,000 titles. As so many libraries did 12 years ago, Providence automated its circulation activities first without much thought about other aspects or uses that could be made of the data. When the library began automated circulation control, only short records were entered; they were not adequate for a catalog for many reasons, among which was the fact that no subject access and little descriptive cataloging was provided. In 1981, expanded title records were entered for all new items. However, for a catalog the data was still inadequate. For PPL this RECON project is the means to have an accurate database for its Public Access Catalog. At the same time, the PPL is reclassifying all the holdings to the LC classification system. That will make future cataloging much easier and less costly, i.e., there will be no more need for customized cataloging. Since a database existed that had been built in Providence over a 10 year period, the PPL began seeking a means to convert these records using the least amount of staff time. In discussing this project with bibliographic utility vendors over the past two years, it became obvious that one vendor could do the job with the criterion we established, i.e., that we use our database and expand it to full MARC records on the equipment we had with as little manual labor as possible. UTLAS was able to work with our automation vendor, CLSI, and come up with a proposal to retrospectively convert our records to machine readable form.

All the libraries that participate in Providence's system are included in this project and their records are also being converted. There are currently 15 other public libraries of varying sizes participating through the Cooperating Libraries Automated Network (CLAN). In addition to converting each library's records, UTLAS will be retained as the authority control in the future. What started as Providence's plan to automate circulation and provide a Public Access Catalog has now become a cataloging source for over one-third of the public libraries.

Providence will continue to use MINI-MARC until all of its branches have an adequate number of public access terminals. At that time, the card catalog will be closed and eventually removed. Members of CLAN will make their own decisions regarding whether or not to create a Public Access Catalog. Most have already indicated they plan to close their catalogs. The time-frame to completion is projected at less than two years.

## OCLC RE-ENTERS

Within the past year the Rhode Island State Library has funded Providence for membership in OCLC/NELINET to use the ILL subsystem. This will end blind searching. PPL's Shared Resources Department, upon receipt of ILL requests, will use OCLC to search the holdings of Rhode Island members and locate specific items. Previously, requests were sent to libraries based on PPL's determination of their strengths. There the items were searched in the local catalog. Sometimes the items were found and sometimes they were not. The State Library believed this blind searching was too costly. In addition to using the OCLC ILL subsystem, the PPL will soon have dial up access to the databases of Rhode Island's OCLC members to determine the status of items requested, i.e., whether they are on the shelf or in circulation.

Over the years computerized operations at the Providence Public Library have changed as needs have changed. The early belief that once an automated system was in place, it was there to stay no longer holds sway. Surely the PPL's electronic configuration will change as much in the succeeding 10 years as it has in the past.

## REFERENCES

Sager, Donald J. "Library Automation for the Urban Public Library." In: Alex Ladenson, Editor, *Current Trends in Library Automation*. Chicago: Urban Libraries Council, 1981, p. 5.

For Product Safety Concerns and Information please contact our EU
representative  GPSR@taylorandfrancis.com
Taylor & Francis Verlag GmbH, Kaufingerstraße 24, 80331 München, Germany

www.ingramcontent.com/pod-product-compliance
Lightning Source LLC
Chambersburg PA
CBHW052134300426

44116CB00010B/1903